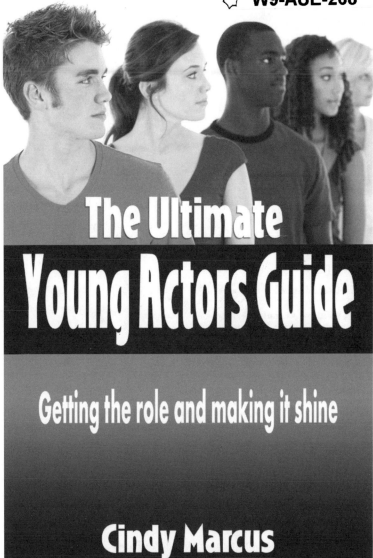

The Ultimate
Young Actors Guide

Getting the role and making it shine

Cindy Marcus

MERIWETHER PUBLISHING LTD.
Colorado Springs, Colorado

Meriwether Publishing Ltd., Publisher
PO Box 7710
Colorado Springs, CO 80933-7710

www.meriwether.com

Editor: Theodore O. Zapel
Assistant editor: Amy Hammelev
Cover design: Jan Melvin

Library of Congress Cataloging-in-Publication Data

Marcus, Cindy.
  The ultimate young actors guide : getting the role and making it shine / by Cindy Marcus. -- 1st ed.
      p. cm.
   ISBN 978-1-56608-179-5
   1. Acting--Vocational guidance--Juvenile literature. I. Title.
   PN2055.M265 2011
   792.02'8--dc23
                                        2011019310

1   2   3   11   12   13

For all my kids,
but especially
Finn, Eliana, James T, and Nicholas

Table of Contents

Foreword

If you're about to read this book, chances are you're a teenager who knows they're ready to learn what it takes to be an actor. I admire you already for being ahead of the game. When I was in middle school and high school, there weren't really any "how to" guides to teach me about what I was sure I wanted to do. In hindsight, you'd think I would have come up with the idea of an entertaining and informative Stanislavsky for Teens, especially after suffering through *An Actor Prepares* in college, required reading that only served to send my eyes rolling upward and my forehead thumping into the spine of the book.

Currently, I am both a real mom and a fake TV mom, which means many teenagers confide their deepest hopes to me as aspiring performers. Generally they go something like this: "I want to be on TV and I want to be famous." Hmm, did I say deep? That's about as deep as the plastic turtle swimming pool you still have in your backyard collecting mosquito water. When I was training, it was more likely that a theatre student would announce, "Someday, I want to be a great actor," the idea being that great actors were working actors. Today, admittedly, many young careers are launched with dizzying speed, and, as I've been told, "Acting doesn't really require any studying, ya fake TV mom." To which I reply, "Hey, kids, you will build nothing lasting from a weird bad haircut or a video of you hitting a tree on a Slip 'n Slide." The more you study what it takes to be a working actor, the better chance you'll have. And that's where *The Ultimate Young Actors Guide* comes in.

An especially helpful section is the one on improvisation. I performed for five years with L.A.'s Groundlings Theatre, and if you can be comfortable with all styles of improv, you'll have the flexibility you need for auditions. You need to learn lines the way they're written, but be versatile enough to deal with new ideas when they're thrown at you. The ability to improvise creates opportunities less prepared actors will miss.

Finally, most of the successful young actors I've had the chance to work with in the past few years have not only been talented, but have been fun, normal, enjoyable people to be around. So, be pleasant, learn everything you can about being an actor, and try, try, try, because so many acting opportunities will not go exactly the way you expect. If all else fails, change your name to Willow.

One of my favorite quotes from a young actor was, "I want to be an actor on TV, but I have a really hard time remembering lines." That's the equivalent of someone saying they want to be a world-class chef but they were born without taste buds, or they want to sing but can't really hear what key the music is in or ... you get the idea. Using this book, study, enjoy every aspect of acting, and, um, do people still say this? Break a leg.

— Mary Scheer, actress/writer
    iCarly, The Penguins of Madagascar, MADtv

Acknowledgments

It takes a village to raise a child and a team to see a dream come true:

Flip, Dennis, Domenic —
my boys; thanks for pushing me outside that comfort zone
and making me always better.

Rebecca, Michele, Ann, and Brad —
thanks for believing in the dream even when it's hard.

Milt and Mickey —
my "parents," you make all people prettier. Including me.

Tammy and Scott and Amber —
my MO "family." I'm so grateful for you.

Pat and Les; Desma; JR and Tina —
"super parents" so does not describe how amazing you are.

Mike B and Troy D —
my MO boys; thanks for taking up the gauntlet.

Carla —
my Shafter girl; thanks for being the visionary teacher that you are.

Glenn —
thanks bud for sharing your home and heart and wife.

Wendy —
thanks for sharing Dennis.

Candy and Clint —
thanks for always coming through

Diane and Leah and Ray K —
thanks for the spark that ignited the fire.

All the Showdown teens —
without you there would be no me.

Lois and Ray and Ted R —
you are the reason I want to do this work.

Amy H —
I just love that you're my editor. Thanks for being there.

Art and Mark and Ted —
Aaaach. Without you this book would never be.
And my dreams would not have come true. You are the best.

Ruth and Sy —
I miss you.

Scott, Jeff, and Tami —
thanks for always staying in the canoe with me.

Flip —
my partner in all things; you are my dream.

And Finn —
You are amazing. A son beyond all measure.
Because of you I can fly.

Introduction

You are an actor if ...

Terror. Joy. Despair. You go to places inside yourself that most people fear.

You celebrate what others dismiss.

You are a child in a world of way too many grown-ups.

You often stand alone 'cause you see life like nobody else.

You love the lights and the laughter and the bows.

You'd rather be in front of a camera or on a stage than anywhere else on the planet.

Dear actor, this book is written for you; its purpose is to celebrate *you.* Nowhere in its pages will you be told "don't be an actor, it's impractical, not sensible, only for the perfect, you can't, you shouldn't ... "

Au contraire.

This book was written to encourage you. You are capable. You are talented. You are smart. You picked up this book didn't you? And if you truly want to be an actor, you can be. Welcome home.

This Book

Unlike most acting tomes, this book was written for teens. Teens question, dream passionately, seek great inner quests, and are still brave enough to behave like children.

Me

Hard to believe, but a very long time ago I was a teen just like you. I loved doing theatre. I thought I wanted to be an actress so my mom signed me up for this summer camp called the Teenage Drama Workshop. Scared was I, but I went. And I am so glad I did; the experience changed my life. I went back for three summers, that's how much I loved it.

Many years later, after many years of success in Hollywood, I met a young teen who felt lost. Listening to her, I realized I felt lost too. Here I had this great career, but my life felt empty. It was time for me to pay it forward ...

Showdown

With the help of a great friend and my wonderful husband, I started a teen theatre program just like the one I'd gone to as a teen. My acting approach was similar to what I'd learned at the Teenage Drama Workshop. And it worked for a while. But I soon realized that times had changed and if I was going to teach the teens, my approach needed to evolve too. Together, the teens and I tried out new exercises. Some were horrible mistakes but most worked better than we could have imagined. Eventually my acting approach became kind of like this living thing, growing and changing as the teens grew and changed. It was really cool.

The camp became known as Showdown. It's national and it's been going on for almost ten years now. Hundreds of teens over the years have walked through Showdown's doors. You could say that my acting approach was created with teens just like you; their passion and dreams and ideas are all over these pages.

The Showdown acting approach is focused on self-exploration. Showdown's philosophy is the more you know about who you are, the more you have to bring to the role ... and life. How can you play someone else if you don't know who you are? How can you convey an emotion if you're not in touch with that emotion?

The Showdown motto is *"Dare to Suck!"* In other words, take a risk. Embrace mistakes, 'cause you learn what not to do in the future. Embrace adventure. Life is not a dress rehearsal. We want you to try things, learn from those experiences, then apply that wonderful knowledge to your character. Life begets art and vice versa.

What's in the Chapters

The chapters in this book cover the A to Zs of technical acting stuff: how to audition, approaching a role (be it musical or not), how to survive the rehearsal process, and what to expect when the show is over.

You will hear from many different directors including Jane Jenkins and her partner Janet Hirschenson, who are *the* casting directors. They discovered Daniel Radcliffe, the actor who plays Harry Potter. Each director has a different approach, but their philosophy is the same: know who you are.

Games

To fully integrate what you're learning, there are games to play in every chapter. *Warning:* the games can make you feel weird. I get that. But you're an actor, so pretend that it doesn't. Play the role of a scientist, learning about acting, not a clown looking to entertain. I promise if you take the games seriously, you'll have more fun and learn a whole bunch more.

Treats along the Way

What fun is it to work without reward? Really. Who wants to do that? So as you read through the book there will be "goodies." I'm not with you in person, so this is my way of pretending that we're together and I'm giving you a cookie or a hug.

 **GOLD STAR**

This is for when you do something brave; you stepped outside your comfort zone. On page 116, you will find a star with "jewels" in it. When you get a Gold Star you will go to page 116 and color in a jewel. Eventually, your star will be a colorful testament to your courage. Yay for you!

This is given to you when it's time for a break. You've been working hard doing the exercises and you need to go out and relax. Treat yourself to something delish. Personally, I love Starbucks' mochas with soy and whip.

This rather geeky, but terribly important reward is given to you when you've done an awesome job. There is a calendar at the back of this book on page 117. It's called the "Uh-Huh I'm Bad, Calendar." When you have an "I'm Bad" moment, which is actually when you've done something great, you mark it in the calendar at the back of the book. You are going to have several, my friend, and by the end of this book you gonna be de baddest cat in de whole darn town.

There's other junk too. Well, not really junk, but extra stuff like …

Aha Moment!

So what's an Aha Moment? Good question. An Aha Moment is an epiphany. Like the proverbial lightbulb going off over your head. It's a realization and it's so important, I don't want you to miss it, so I repeat it to make sure you got it. Get that?

Trivia

It could be true, maybe not, either way it's fun to share with friends at a party.
Since the best way to learn is through experience, let's jump right in...

Chapter One

Who Are You?

*"There is a vitality, a life force, an energy, a quickening that is translated
through you into action, and there is only one of you in all of time.
This expression is unique, and if you block it, it will never exist through
any other medium and be lost."*
— Martha Graham

*"In this galaxy there's a mathematical probability of three million
Earth-type planets. And in the universe, three million galaxies like this.
And in all that, and perhaps more ... only one of each of us."*
— Dr. McCoy, Star Trek, "Balance of Terror"

There is only one you. Think about that. In all of time and creation, never again will your special gifts come our way. Whoa. You are *that* important.

So who are you? What makes you special? What is uniquely you? You cannot manifest that awesomeness that is you if you don't know who "you" is. So you must find out what makes you tick.

 Aha Moment!

Actors draw from themselves to create a memorable character. The more you know about yourself, the more you will have to draw on. In other words, the more you know about you, the more you will have in your inner arsenal to help you create an incredible character. So make it your mission to find out who you are!

Be Your Own Observer

Do you remember doing science fair projects in fifth grade? You'd ask questions like how does a lightbulb work or what can make a volcano erupt? Then you'd state your hypothesis and investigate and then offer a conclusion.

Well, you need to look at your life with the same care as you examined those scientific questions. So like the lightbulb, what ignites your light? And what extinguishes it? Like the volcano, what makes you erupt? What are you willing to sacrifice to squelch the flame inside?

I Feel

If you've never thought about what matters to you, the best way to learn is to listen to your feelings. What makes you happy, angry, or sad? Feelings are like a map to your heart. And they're easy to notice once you learn the right questions to ask. Are you ready? The question is ... how do I feel?

That's it. Pretty simple, huh? You ask yourself, "How do I feel?"

However, you want to be specific. No vague answers like, "I'm OK" or "I'm all right," or "Yeah, I'm good." Answers like that won't tell you much. And remember, the goal here is to find out as much as you can about you. So use specific feelings. I'm angry. I'm frustrated. I feel joyous. I feel lethargic.

Good job. Now, once you've established what you're feeling, note where you place that feeling in your body. Does this make sense? Let me explain ... sometimes when I'm tired I feel fatigue behind my eyes, other times it's this knot in my chest. Tired can come from many different places and where the tired comes from denotes what kind of tired it is. So, if I'm sleepy-tired, it's definitely behind my eyes 'cause they want to close. If I'm fatigue-tired 'cause I've been working too much, I would feel achy all over. If I'm upset-tired 'cause I've been arguing with my husband, it's that knot in my chest. Knowing where you physically place your feelings can help you conjure them up later. So make note of the physical sensation and move on to asking yourself, "Why?"

Why do I feel this way? Why do I love caramel sauce but hate hot fudge? Why do I love running in the rain, but hate taking showers? Do you see? Ask yourself why. Why do you feel tired? Why are you so angry?

Why is an awesome question to ask yourself 'cause it can take you to deeper and deeper levels of you. Let me show you what I mean ...

"Cindy, how do you feel?"

I'm so glad you asked, dear actor/reader, I'll tell you, "I feel excited and a little nervous."

"Why do you feel excited and nervous, Cindy?"

"I feel excited because I'm getting to share all of this with you, nervous 'cause what if you don't like it?"

Whoa. That just told me a lot about me, didn't it? It told me that I like teaching acting — I was excited. And that your feelings matter to me 'cause I was nervous you might not like what I have to say. The nervous feeling was in my stomach, by the way, and the excited was in my face — I found myself wanting to smile.

Now your turn. How do you feel?

 Aha Moment!

Feelings are neither good nor bad. They are simply feelings. So please don't judge them. You feel angry. Anger may feel uncomfortable, but it's not a bad feeling. It's information. Like if I were to tell you that if you step into a puddle your feet get wet. I'm not bad or good, I'm just relaying information. What you chose to do about the information is up to you. The same is true with your feelings. They are guideposts informing you of whether you wish to continue what you're doing or not. *So just note the feeling and move on.*

You can share your feelings with your friends or you can keep them to yourself, that's up to you. But not wanting to share and/or wanting to share tells you something about you and your friends, doesn't it? Hmmmm.

"Ah just act the way ah feel."
— Elvis Presley

The You Game

Let's play a new game. (I love this one). This one will actually require some props.

You will need:

1. Lots of old magazines you can rip up. Hopefully different kinds of magazines. Not just *In Style* or *People*, but a variety, even magazines you'd never read in a million years. Just lots and lots of magazines. You can get mags really cheap at the library. Just ask the librarian where the Friends of the Library book sale racks in the library are and you'll find like a bazillion of them.

11

2. A large space to spread out.
3. A five-minute timer.
4. Your iPod or computer or whatever device you play to hear music.
5. An 8½ by 11 piece of poster board.
6. A glue stick.

Directions:
1. Find a big spot on the floor where you and your magazines can spread out. Now fan the magazines out around you. Pretend you're the center of a flower and the mags are your petals. All around.
2. Set the timer for five minutes.
3. Now open the magazines and rip out any pictures or phrases or words that speak to you. Have fun with this. Don't be all neat. Tear away.
4. When the timer dings, put the pics and phrases you ripped out in one neat pile and then everything else that is left over in another pile.
5. Put on your music.
6. Take a look at the pictures you chose. What pops out at you? Did you rip ten pictures of cars? Did you respond to certain words? Any images that surprise you? Pull out any image or word that doesn't speak to you or feels redundant. Put those in with the unused pile.
7. Now create a collage of the images and words you liked on the poster board. Place them however you wish.
8. Admire your collage.

The You Game: The Sequel

Another way to play the collage game is to rip and collage with a phrase in mind.

You will need:
All the same stuff as The You Game.

Directions:
1. Lay out magazines.
2. Set the timer for five minutes.
3. As you are ripping, think of this phrase, "I wish ... "
4. Once the timer dings, it's time to look at your images and see what pops out at you.
5. Then collage or not, that's up to you.

You can do a collage for lots of different phases:
I regret …
My epitaph will say …
I hate …

The You Game: The Final Chapter

This is also an amazing character exercise. In this version, you do everything as you've done before, but the question you ask yourself is: What does my character's home look like? Another question could be: What is my character's work life like? Or maybe: What is my character's family tree? You get the idea how to do this, right?

Darlin', you've done your work. It's time to take a break. Go out and treat yourself to something delish. Is it ice cream? Coffee? A glass of milk and a cookie? Great job.

Chapter Two

Sense and Sense-ability

We have five glorious senses. Five! Taste. Touch. Smell. Hear. See. Wow. How cool is that? But how often do we emphasize one sense over another? Think about it. Don't you rely on your sight when other senses can be just as wonderful? When was the last time you smelled an amazing painting instead of simply gazed at it or listened to a starry night? The goal of this chapter is to rediscover all your amazing senses.

Sound

Ah, hearing. What an amazing piece of machinery are the ears.

Trivia

Teens can hear sounds that adults (over twenty-five) can't. 'Tis true. Adults usually can't hear above 25kHz. In addition, listening to an iPod for extended periods of time can damage your ears. If you want to know more cool ear facts, go to www.noiseaddicts.com.

Perhaps the best way to appreciate hearing is to take it away, yes? So I want you to take a moment and imagine that you can't hear. What would you miss out on? Music. Oh no, I would hate not being able to hear music. Music is so comforting. And when I'm livid angry, listening to AC/DC totally rocks. I crank them up and feel so justified in my livitude. And what about laughter? If I couldn't hear, I'd never again hear the sound of my son's giggles. That would be horrible.

I love my ears, even if I can't hear above 25kHz. They're awesome. And now knowing I want to appreciate my ability to hear, I'm going to practice listening. Are you?

Aha Moment!

Great acting comes from great listening.

Acting is about listening. But let me be clear, listening does not mean, "Oh I heard you speak and now it's my turn to say my line." Truly listening is to hear *their* feelings behind *their* words, not *your* feelings behind *their* words — the emotions of the person who is speaking. Whoa. Think about that. When was the last time you listened without letting your mind wander or thinking about your next line or noting how what they're saying makes you feel? When was the last time you just listened to your acting partner or friend or parent without any kind of judgment? Try that. But I warn you, great listening is a lot easier said than done.

Sssshhhh

Purpose of the game:

It's pretty much as it sounds. You don't speak. You shhhh, so that you may listen.

Directions:

1. Choose an allotted period of time. I suggest no more than an hour.
2. Go to a place where there are people: school, home, the mall.
3. Don't speak. Listen.

Now some of you will bring a pad of paper and pen so you can write what you have to say. *Don't!* And don't do charades or semaphore or anything silly you can think of to communicate. Because this game is not about not speaking, it's about listening — so sssshhhh and listen.

You'll hear a secret conversation or a unique sound or just your own thoughts. Note them. And keep listening until the time is up.

Warning: you may not play this game as an excuse to not participate in class. Nuh-uh. Snap. Snap. Oh, and no sitting and listening to your iPod for an hour.

Music

Purpose of the game:
Listen to many different kinds of music.

Directions:
Did you know the library lets you check out CDs? Uh-huh. They do. For the price of a library card (which should be free) you can check out as many CDs as you dream.

1. I want you to go to the library and pick out five different kinds of music CDs. Ah, but here's the catch: the CDs must be music you'd never think you'd like. Check out opera, classical, world music, jazz, spirituals, oompah — oh the list goes on and on.
2. Now listen to one song from each CD. The trick is listening. Without judgment. Stay open. See if you actually like the music. I made myself listen to Flogging Molly and I loved it. Really.

Aliens

Purpose of the game:
Listen to the sound of voices and not the words.

Directions:

1. Go to the mall, the airport, the bus station, or a restaurant. Any place where you can comfortably eavesdrop on another conversation.
2. Pretend you are an alien from another planet and you don't understand anything anyone is saying. To you, it's gibberish.
3. Listen to the conversation. But remember, don't listen to the words they are saying. Listen as if the voices were instruments in a classical piece of music, and the instruments can't use words. They can only use their sound to convey emotion and story. Yes? An example of what I might hear in a conversation was one voice was low pitched or deep and resonant but spoke quickly and the other voice was high and skittered. The tone was sharp 'cause the voices sounded almost discordant. Make sense?
4. Note what emotion you think is passing between those in the conversation. And is the emotion the same for each voice? Do you recognize the emotion in yourself?
5. Walk away.
6. Mimic the voices you've heard.

 **GOLD STAR**

For trying out all of the games and learning a bit more about yourself.

Yay for you! Go to the back of the book, color in a star. Any color you like. It's your star.

 Aha Moment!

Your senses are a ticket to your memories.

Do you find that listening to a certain song can catapult you back to another time in your life? Like instant time travel, the tune has sent you to a time that doesn't exist anymore? For example, you're in your bedroom listening to Jethro Tull and then suddenly your mind takes you to the backseat of a car and you're on a vacation with your parents. Sounds, smells, tastes can return you to past moments in your life. Learning to use your "sense memories" is a great acting tool.

Taste

Sweet. Salty. Bitter. Aren't our taste buds awesome? And our mouth, I mean what it can do. A mouth can chew our food and make it into fuel. Wow. We have lips that can smile and frown and kiss. Whoa. Plus without our mouth, how would we speak? Or how would we breathe if we had a cold?

But my personal fave is eating. So hang on, you're about to take your taste buds on a journey 'round the world!

Cuisine de World

Purpose of the game:
Taste foods from around the world.

Directions:
You play this game in two phases. In Phase One, you will read a list of foods and figure out where the foods come from. In Phase Two you will eat the foods.

Phase One

1. Read the list of foods below.
2. Next to the food, write what country you think it's from.
3. Check to see how many you got right with the answers at the end of the list. (Oh, and no peeking!)
    a. Pad Thai
    b. Gefilte Fish
    c. Stollen
    d. Naan
    e. Jambalaya
    f. Haggis
    g. Tempura
    h. Borscht
    i. Chim Cut Ro-Ti
    j. Cou-cou
    k. Go Lo Yuk
    l. Pandekager
    m. Pain Perdu
    n. Pasta e Fagioli
    o. Sofrito
    p. Falafel
    q. Rugelach
    r. Grits
    s. Paella
    t. Burrito

Answers: a. Thailand b. Germany c. Germany d. Persia e. Louisiana f. Scotland g. Japan h. Ukraine i. Vietnam j. Caribbean k. China l. Denmark m. France n. Italy o. Cuba p. Middle East q. Poland r. The American South s. Spain t. Mexico

Phase Two
1. Total the points you got right.
2. Check to see what kind of foodie you are from the list below.
3. Follow the eating instructions.

16-20 points: World Traveler. Your taste buds have traveled a bit. Taste two of the above dishes.

11-15 points: Happy Camper. Your taste buds have been 'round the block, but not much farther. Taste three of the above dishes.

6-10 points: Local Yokel. Your taste buds need some experience. Taste at least five of the above dishes.

0-5 points: Couch Potato. Friend, we need to get you up and moving. Taste at least seven of the above dishes.

So what did you learn about yourself? You like Thai food but Mexican makes you gag? You love Falafel but not a Gefilte Fish fan? Cool. Congrats. What will you sample next? Go on, you can even try something from off the list.

Remember our goal: to taste life, so we can learn who and what we are, so we have that much more to bring to the character we're playing.

It's time to taste life. Eat, drink, and merriness. Crunch a carrot, partake of a parsnip, tear at a tomato, or sample a sardine.

Sight

I don't know if it's good or bad, but I have to say that sight is probably the "Big Gun" of the senses. It's the power player, because sight is the sense most people rely on.

"The enemy of Creativity is the absence of limitation."
— Orson Wells

19

Aha Moment!

Part of being a great actor is making great choices. And making good choices requires that you understand you made the choice. Nobody held a gun to your head and told you to behave this way. You chose to act as you did. The sooner you understand and accept this, the freer you will be because the world will then be something you chose. Does this make sense?

Said another way, you are responsible for everything you do. Whatever you put into your body. Whatever you say. You make that happen and nobody else.

Let me be more specific. I'm encouraging you to go out and sample life. Does this mean you should go out and try drugs? Alcohol? Running across a train track? No. Make a *good* choice. You're a capable, brilliant, talented person. You can choose the best thing for you. Or not. That's up to you.

The Blind Game

Purpose of the game:

To build trust as you live without your sight.

Directions:

1. You will need a blindfold and a partner.
2. Choose one person to be the Guide and one person to be the Blind.
3. "Blind" puts the blindfold on.
4. Guide takes Blind on a tour of the neighborhood.
5. Guide must make sure to guide over steps, down driveways, across streets, etc. Guide does this by standing close to Blind, holding Blind at the elbow, using as little speaking as possible.

    Guide's job is also to give Blind a sensory experience. Guide directs Blind to a rough tree trunk and lets Blind feel it without telling Blind what it is (again, don't speak). Guide could also offer up a leaf to smell, walk Blind into dark places and light places, and walk Blind over grass, pavement, or stone.

    It is really important that you speak as little as possible. Silence is golden.

6. Now Guide and Blind switch. Blind becomes the seeing Guide while Guide becomes Blind by putting the blindfold on. There is no time limit to this game. Play for as long or as little as you like. Switch roles as often as you both feel comfortable. Just remember that there's little talking while you're playing.

7. When you have finished playing, share what you realized. You'll be surprised how much more to this game there was than just not seeing. Issues of trust come up. And fear. It's amazing.

Touch

As sight tends to be our number one sense, touch often gets overlooked. When was the last time you actually savored the coolness of your sheets as you fell into bed? Or touched all the nooks and crannies of your face instead of just glared at those "flaws"?

Take a moment now and feel the texture of your hair. What does it feel like? Is your hair thick or thin? Coarse or soft? Wet or dry? Scrunch your hair. Flatten your mane. Twirl the hair through your fingertips. Note how you feel doing this. Weird? Interested? Bored? Oh, more information about you. Why do you feel this way? Hmmmm.

Go Rogue

Purpose of the game:
Like Rogue in *X-Men,* live wearing gloves for a day.

Directions:
1. Get a pair of gloves. The gloves can be lace, cotton, spandex, etc. It's up to you.
2. Put the gloves on when you wake in the morning. Except during "Challenge Times," do not take the gloves off until the end of the day.
3. "Challenge Times" are going to the bathroom, washing dishes, taking a shower, or anything that requires your hands to be in water. At that time, you may take the gloves off. Note how it feels not to have to wear the gloves. Is it a relief? Is it disappointing?

Fabric

Purpose of the game:
Feel different types of fabric.

Directions:
1. With a friend or partner, go to your local fabric store.
2. Feel ten different types of fabrics: satin, lace, velvet, fur, leather, leatherette, cotton, wool, flannel, silk.
3. After you've felt all the fabrics, close your eyes.
4. While your eyes are closed, have your friend guide you through the fabric store, letting you touch the different fabrics.
5. With eyes still closed, guess which fabric is which just by the feel.

Smell

I think in many ways smell is the most profound of the senses.

Trivia
Did you know that early humans didn't have noses, they had holes? Oh, and babies use their sense of smell to find their mother's breast. And here's my personal fave, women still use smell to determine their potential mates? Weird, huh?

From a totally personal POV, sometimes I'd rather smell than taste. The deep, warm aroma of coffee intrigued me long before I started drinking my mochas. The rich, sweet scent of chocolate often satisfies me enough that I don't buy.

Smells can offend. Scent can attract. Our noses do rock.

Smell First

Purpose of the game:
Get into your more primal side.

Directions:
This game might feel a bit weird, so maybe warn your friends you've gone primitive.
1. For one day, smell whatever you encounter first, before you eat or speak or do. So if you see your buddy at school, smell him, then say "hi." You are having cereal for breakfast, smell the spoonful then dig in. If you're a metro-sexual and into lotion, smell before you rub it on your face. You get the picture. Yes?

2. Note which scents made you happy and which make you sad and what scent took you down memory lane. This is very important, so I'm going to repeat it, *note which of the scents took you down memory lane.* We're going to work with the memory sense connection in the next chapter and I want you to remember.

Sensory Overload?

We've only just begun exploring your senses. Wait till you see what we got planned for you in Chapter Three!

Uh-Huh I'm BAD! You bad. Uh-huh. Mark this day on the calendar in the back.

Chapter Three

Thanks for the Memories

This chapter is devoted to taking all those lovely new senses you've just relearned to love and use them to build a memory.

What's Your Life Story

If I were to ask you who you are, what would you say now? Would you include all your new likes and dislikes? Would you state the facts? "Well, I was born in a small log cabin in Illinois." (Wait, that's Abe Lincoln.) What else would you include?

Take a moment and think about it. What comes up for you?

You might share your passions and a fact or two. But somewhere in that stew we call you, there's still one thing missing, and that's your memories. It might be when you learned to ride a bike or got your first kiss. The crush that got away or the one that didn't. Your memories and the feelings you associated with them help define who you are. I might even go so far as to say they are the reason you behave the way you do. Let me explain …

When I was nine, my parents dragged me to the Santa Monica Playhouse. OMG. That tiny event changed the direction of my life forever. You see, the owner of the theatre, Ted Rotter — this short, dark, and handsome Belgian — paid special attention to me. Nobody had ever understood me the way he did. Not even my parents. He seemed to understand my nine-year-old hopes and dreams before I even said them. I loved going to the playhouse. It was the first time I knew home. Since that fateful winter when I walked through the doors of the playhouse and met Ted, I've adored being in a theatre. I would rather be there than anywhere on the planet. Theatres are my happy place. And if I have a choice to do theatre or, say, go on a trip, boy I'd be hard-pressed to choose which I would prefer. That's how much I love being in a theatre. And that event, going to the playhouse, has infused most of the choices I make to this day. That memory is so joyous I seek out other opportunities to do shows. Does that make sense? Had I hated going to the theatre, I would not have gone on to do more. And I probably would not have met my husband, who I met doing a show. I wouldn't be writing this book.

Now to clarify, a memory itself isn't good or bad. It's just a memory. It's how we feel about the memory that gives it importance in our lives.

However, every memory matters when you are an actor. Let's say you're going to play a killer. Oh dear, you've never done that, right? So how would you know what feelings a killer had? Oh wait, maybe you have acted with murderous rage. Have you ever stomped a cockroach? Crushed a spider? At the time you did those evil deeds you probably didn't notice that it would matter in later acting years. You just saw an ugly bug and *stomp!* destroyed its hideous life. But to play a murderous teen, that seemingly inconsequential moment is now mondo important. You'll need it to conjure up the desire to kill for the play. You see how every memory is useful? And it's important you know how to tap into memories and make them work for you.

> *"Acting is a question of absorbing other people's personalities*
> *and adding some of your own experience."*
> — Paul Newman

Memory Games

Autobiographer You

Purpose of the game:
Write a memory.

Directions:
1. You will need a pad of paper, a pen, a ten-minute timer.
2. Set the timer for twenty minutes. Don't worry if you can't get everything down in the time allotted. Just write what you can.
3. Think of a memory. Putting on music can sometimes inspire you. Put pen to paper and write the memory. Remember to include those amazing five senses. What sounds were going on? What taste was in your mouth? Was it sweet or sour or salty? What about touch? What about smells? Was it near an ocean? Beside an oil well and reeked of burnt rubber? What did the space look like?
5. After the timer dings, go get yourself a treat.

Time for a bit of comfort food from your childhood. Peanut butter and jelly? Grilled cheese with a pickle on the side? Red Jell-o with lots of whip cream? Make a whip cream mustache!

6. While you're sipping that hot cocoa or munching on your PB and J, reread what you've written. Note how it makes you feel. Are there more pieces to the memory you wish to add? Do so. Reading the memory, does it connect you to other memories? You can write those too if you like, but you don't have to. The choice is yours.

OK, so did you like writing? Hate it? Remember, everything we do is a tool for you to learn more about yourself. So how do you feel about writing your memories? Would you rather write fictional stories? Do you feel inspired to write your autobiography? Why? Huh. And hmmmm.

A Character's Story

Let's move on to your next step.

Every character you play is just like you in that he has passions and idiosyncrasies, memories and ailments — he is a living, breathing being. And it's up to you, the actor, to make that character come to life. But to do that, you must ground your character's life in your life. Use your memories, feelings, and thoughts to make the character real. Does this make sense? You are the conduit that channels the character. You are the breath to the character's life. You are the source.

The first step to uncovering your character's life is to go to the script. The script will give you both hard facts about your character and implicative information. Let me explain ... in the musical *Fiddler on the Roof,* it's a fact that Tevye wants to be rich 'cause he sings, "I Want to Be A Rich Man." You see, it's clearly stated. However, it's implied that Tevye dearly loves his daughters, because he's willing to risk tradition for the love of his daughters. Nowhere in the script does Tevye say, "I love my daughters." We just know this because of his actions. It's up to you, detective/actor person, to decipher the script's clues.

Script Clues

We are going to walk through an example of finding clues in a script to uncover a character.

You will need the book to *The Sound of Music*. You can find it at the library. Or if worse comes to worse, rent the movie. Also helpful is a pen and pad of paper.

First, read the script once through for enjoyment. Now read the script looking for Maria clues. As you find a clue, write it down on your pad.

Great job. Big hug.

Here are some clues you might have missed: What year did her story take place? What was the setting? What was the overall tone of the play?

Awesome job, honeycomb! What did you learn about Maria? I'll tell you what I got, and you see if you agree …

Maria is a positive person (she turns a scary storm into a slumber party). She's an orphan (that's a fact given to us). She loves the Sisters and feels safe with them (she runs back to them when she's scared). She marches to her own drum (she should be in class but she's off in the hills singing). She knows how to sew (that's a fact 'cause she takes the curtains down and makes clothes). She loves the mountains (learned that from the song "The Hills Are Alive"). She loves kids and knows how to handle them (she gets hired as a nanny and they don't scare her away). She lived in the '30s (a fact). She's from Austria (a fact).

So what clues did you find?

Bridging the Memories

Now you have a skeleton of Maria, but you need to add in all the flesh and hair and stuff if she's going to be a living, breathing human. You do this by attaching your life experiences, your feelings, and your memories to Maria.

At this point in our acting journey, I can't tell you how many of my actors have said to me, "But Cindy, if I use my memories and stuff, then my character won't be different than me. She'll be just like me, and that's not acting." Pish posh! Au contraire, young thespian. The character you are playing doesn't really exist. You must breathe life into her for her to be real. And the only life you have is your own.

All right, so back to Maria. Let's go back to the list I created from the script. *Maria is a positive person.* OK, I'm a pretty positive person so I can easily identify with Maria. I won't need to do a lot of memory excavating to make that part of her real.

27

But what if I wasn't a "glass is half full" kind of girl? What if I was "emo," how do I create a positive Maria then? I would go back into my memory well and remember a time when I was feeling good. Maybe when I listened to a certain song or read a cool poem. Once I have the memory, I'd either make a mental note of that memory or I could write it down next to "Maria is a positive person" in my list. For now, I'll make a mental note and move on to the next item.

Maria is an orphan. Oh dear, I've never been an orphan so I will definitely need to remember a time in my life when I felt orphaned. When I find that memory, I make note or write it down.

Some of the connections between you and your character will come easily. And for some you will have to dig. For example, Maria lived in Nazi-occupied Austria. Phew. That's a toughie. For me, I cannot possibly relate to Maria. I live in the United States. I have never known the occupation of my country. But this is about making Maria real, so I'm going to have to dig for memories that are close to her experience. Here's what I came up with: I have lived under presidencies where I completely disagreed and under regimes that terrified me. I'll make a note of a period in my history when I felt truly terrified of losing my freedoms.

What about Maria's hills? I've never seen the Swiss Alps, but I do live near the Santa Monica Mountains and I love them. I actually breathe easier every time I crest the SM Mountains and drive down into my valley. To connect with Maria I will remember a day when the sky was crystal blue and I felt particularly happy looking at my mountains.

Do you see how this works? Do you see now why you need to know about yourself? Every part of you can be used as a tool to build a character. And if you don't know who you are, you will have nothing to build with. You will *play* at Maria, instead of *be* Maria.

Trivia

Elaine Stritch, a Broadway icon, aka Jack Donaghy's mother on *30 Rock*, was doing Sondheim's *Company*. Her song was "Ladies Who Lunch." And she was up onstage singing, giving the song everything inside her soul and more. She finished the song and ... silence. Not a peep. The audience was silent. Can you say "check, please"? Elaine was mortified. Then ... came the applause. Thunderous cheers!

You see, what happened was the audience was so carried away by Stritch's reality, they lost theirs. They were lost in her world and forgot their own. When they realized who they were, they screamed and cheered for her.

Elaine eventually became known as the actress who sings, "Ladies Who Lunch."

By now, you've written a list of Maria traits and then tapped your memories in any instance where you couldn't clearly relate to Maria. Wow. That's a lot. Great job.

It's now time to go to the next level.

Remembering Your Memories

Purpose of the game:

Remember the feeling associated with a memory.

Directions:

You will need a comfortable chair and two kinds of music. You'll need peaceful, relaxing music and a song that reminds you of another time in your life.

1. Put on the relaxing music.
2. Sit in the chair.
3. Completely relax. Feet are flat on the floor. Arms are uncrossed with hands either on your lap or on the arms of the chair. Head is resting comfortably against the back of the chair. Eyes are closed. Take three deep breaths. Easy breath in and easy breath out.

    Now go through every part of your body and focus on relaxing it. You do this by breathing into that part of the body. Relax your eyes. If you feel tension there, breathe into it. Now relax your mouth then your neck. Just work from head to toe, breathing in relaxation, breathing out any tension.
4. Once you've relaxed completely, we want to take that relaxation to the next level. You do this by tightening different parts of your body and then relaxing them. So you tighten your face. Scrunch, scrunch, scrunch it up. Now relax. Do the same thing with your neck. Tighten, tighten, tighten. Let go. You do this with each part of your body, from top to bottom.
5. Put on the song that reminds you of a memory.
6. Focus on the memory.
7. Let the music take you back in time to that moment. Now, using all your senses, relive it. Begin with sight. What do you see? What colors? What people? What are their expressions? How do their expressions make you feel? Tense. Excited. Sad. Go to sound. What do you hear? The song for sure, but how does the tune make you feel? What other sounds exist? Taste. What's the

taste in your mouth? Is it burning and coppery or sweet and pleasant? Fully taste that taste and notice how it makes you feel. Touch. What does the air feel like? What sensations tickle your skin? How does that feel? Let every sense explode within you until you feel you are there.

8. Now remember the feeling associated with this memory. Remember it fully. If tears come, great. If laughter follows, even better. Whatever it is, don't judge it. Just let it come. Happy. Mad. Sad. Confused. Feel it.

That's it. You did it. You took a memory and you recreated it.

 **GOLD STAR**

For taking a risk. And being willing to really delve into all the parts of you. Yay for you! Go to the back of the book, color a stone any color you like. It's your star.

Applying the Memory

I used this exercise more times than I can count when I was a young actress, and it was hugely successful for me. My process was in three steps. First, about ten to fifteen minutes before I had to go on, I'd find a quiet place to relax. My second step was to close my eyes and recreate whatever memory I felt connected me to my character. The third step was to reconnect with my character. Then I'd go onstage.

Specifically, I played Laura in *Look Homeward, Angel.* What I did was this ... about ten minutes before I'd have to enter, I'd stand in the wings and walk down memory lane. For example, in the play Laura has to say good-bye to her young lover Eugene.

You see, I was sixteen, I didn't have any young lovers or old lovers or even a pet fish to say good-bye to. But Laura still had to be real to the audience so I'd close my eyes and remember saying good-bye to someone *I* dearly loved. In this case, it was my grandfather. I'd remember being at his funeral and feeling so scared. I remembered the way the light hit the grave marker and my father's face as he buried his dad. I remembered the smell of fresh dirt as they lowered the casket in the ground. The way my mouth tasted was salty from tears, yet I didn't cry. I held back, so scared was I to say good-bye. The actress me ran through every sense until I felt like I was actually at my grandfather's burial. Often tears would erupt it felt so real. Once I felt the feelings I thought Laura felt, I'd open my eyes and think about Laura. I'd ask myself, "Where are you, Laura?" Laura would have said, "I'm in the bedroom packing." "What do you want, Laura?" Laura would say, "To stay here forever, but I can't. His mother doesn't accept me." "What do you want in the future, Laura?" Laura might say, "I want to find a love like this again." Now connected with my very real feelings and Laura's reality, I entered the stage.

This process was amazingly successful for me. It worked every time. And I ate up the comments I got from the audience. One man even said I was luminescent. Me? Luminescent? Wow. So use this process if it works for you. I happily share it. But if you find only part is valuable, that's OK too. The point is to find the reality of the character, not how you find it.

Trivia

Dustin Hoffman and Sir Laurence Olivier were in the movie *Marathon Man*. Oh it's a scary flick about Nazi war criminals. Anyway, Dustin Hoffman had a scene with Larry (that's what he let you call him, you know). In one particular scene, Dustin had to have been running when he entered. So to get himself in character, that's what Mr. Hoffman did. He ran. And ran. And ran. Then he'd enter the scene exhausted and winded. Larry once asked Dustin why he went to all that trouble. Dustin's reply was, "I can feel the character this way. What do you do when you want to make something real?" Larry looked at him and said, "I just act, my boy." So two schools of approach, both incredibly valid from Oscar-winning actors — you choose what works for you.

Chapter Four

Auditioning

From the dawn of man to the present day, across all walks of life, there is one universal question that bonds actors across time and space … *why didn't I get the part?* And to this question I have an answer … *getting cast has nothing and everything to do with you.*

This is so important I'm going to repeat it … *getting cast has nothing and everything to do with you.*

I will now say it in Pig Latin … *Ettingay astcay ashay othingnay nday rythingvay otay oday ithway ouyay.*

In Martian? *Bleep, blah xneee … Nah.*

You get the point, right? *Getting cast has nothing and everything to do with you.*

Now let me explain. Getting cast has nothing to do with you because, whether you like it or not, whether you think it's fair or not, directors have something in mind when you step up to audition. And the director is looking for "it" in you. Now, oftentimes the director can't articulate what "it" is. They just know they're looking for "it" and they'll know "it" when they see "it." So it doesn't matter if you stand on your head, offer bribes, or cry. If you don't have that "it" thing, you will not get cast. But that's not all. Getting the role has nothing to do with you 'cause getting a great actor might not be the only thing the director needs to think about. I have worked on movies and shows where lots of other factors come into play. Here are just a few: she's too expensive; she won't work with that actor; the producer wants his cousin, child, or girlfriend; this actor can sell more tickets than that actor; I have little time and lots to do, I need an actor I've worked with before; he won't fit into the costume; she doesn't have enough experience; she has too much experience for this role; her schedule conflicts with mine. And these are just a few of the reasons I have cast and not cast people.

Now the reason that getting cast has everything to do with you is because the only defense you have against this craziness is to be you. Yep, that's what I said. Be yourself.

> *"This above all, to thine own self be true."*
> *— The Bard*
> *aka William Shakespeare*

Aha Moment!

Embrace all that you are and let it shine, because whether or not you get cast, the director will remember you for other future roles *and* you will walk away from the audition feeling really good about yourself, because you knew you were true to you. So *be you!*

An Actor's "Tail"

We were casting Nuka in *The Lion King 2*. Nuka was Kovu — the hero's — second in command. And originally, we were looking for someone to play Nuka as a strong warrior-type. Then Andy Dick walked in.

Now for anyone who knows Andy, nobody could confuse him for a super soldier guy. He's goofy. Funny. And plays neurotic really well. Not anything we saw for Nuka. Then Andy read. And it was like the proverbial light went off over our heads. We realized that Nuka wouldn't be strong, because Mom Zira has neglected him and he feels unloved and jealous. Whoa. Andy's reading made us completely rethink the entire character. Eventually, we rewrote Nuka, and redrew him, giving Andy the part!

Had Andy come in and tried to be something he wasn't, it would have been fine, but we would not have cast him 'cause he wasn't right for the role. But Andy knew who he was, what his strengths were, and let them shine.

" ... Follow your bliss [and] you put yourself on a kind of track
that has been there all the while, waiting for you, and the life that
you ought to be living is the one you are living. When you can see that,
you begin to meet people who are in your field of bliss, and they open
doors to you. I say, follow your bliss and don't be afraid, and doors
will open where you didn't know they were going to be."
— Joseph Campbell

Do you see, my lovely young actor? When you know who you are and you embrace that, "doors will open when you didn't know where they were going to be."

That said, there are some things you can do to help a director see the wonder that is you. There are simple techniques you can apply to give a better audition.

What You Need before You Audition

Trivia
The actresses who got rejected for the part of Buttercup in the movie *The Princess Bride* reads like a "who's who in Hollywood." Here are just a few of the names: Uma Thurman (uh-huh, she was too exotic looking), Courtney Cox (who went on to star in *Friends*), Sarah Jessica Parker, Meg Ryan, and Kyra Sedgewick. And each of these actresses is amazing. They just weren't what the director was looking for. Eventually that part went to Robin Wright, who at the time was dissed 'cause she was a soap actress.

Auditions are like a job interview. The employer (director or casting director) is looking to hire an employee (actor) to do a job.

The typical theatre audition — if there is a typical audition — goes something like this. You walk in. You see other actors who look a lot like you sitting and waiting for their chance to read. (But because you've read this book, you're not worried about those other actors, 'cause you know you have a unique, wonderful quality that will be right or it won't. And you'll walk away making an awesome impression.) You give the person at the desk, sitting by the director, at the door, your headshot and résumé. What is a headshot and résumé? I'm glad you asked.

A Headshot
A headshot is an 8 x 10" picture of you. In the old days, headshots were black and white, but today with the amazing ability of digital, the pics are color. The headshot has your name in a lower corner on the front of the picture; this is so the director can easily put a name with a face when she's reviewing the pictures later on.

A few words about headshots:
1. You want the picture to look like you. Not the glamorized-you or the older-you or the model-you. You.
2. Keep the picture simple. Don't bring in a snapshot from your trip to the Yukon. Just your face, looking at the camera.

3. You can touch up the picture, taking out blemishes, but if you have a birthmark, don't cover it up.
4. Choose a picture that you are excited about. However, once you get an agent or a manager, they may ask you to take different pictures. Do as they ask you to do, but trust what feels right. If the agents want you to use an image that makes you feel uncomfortable, and if they insist and aren't willing to work with you, maybe they're not your right representative?

A Résumé

A *résumé* is a list of all of your actor qualifications. It includes your previous jobs, where you've trained and with who, special skills you might have, your height, weight, and age, and your union affiliations. It covers your previous jobs, training, special skills, and union affiliation.

Previous Jobs

Let's start with *previous jobs.*

Sometimes you don't have any previous jobs. You've just started out. No worries. Have you ever spoken in your classroom? Were you a Hanukkah light for the Winter Show? Put that down. Include the name of the show, what part you played, where you did the show and when. If you're in a show that is unknown, say the name of the show and the type of role you had: minor, featured or lead, and where you did the show.

Trivia

When we were casting *Lord of the Flies* for Castle Rock, the director, Harry Hook — an English bloke — insisted on using unknown actors. He wanted ordinary kids because he felt that would make the movie more real. Rent the movie and decide for yourself if professional actors would have been a better choice.

Training

After *previous jobs,* you will want to include your *training.*

Who have you studied with? What acting coaches? What dance classes have you taken? What about voice lessons? Martial arts? Your training can mean a lot to a director because it shows a couple of things: you care enough to develop your craft when you are not working; you might have skills that you didn't share, but could help with the role; and you might have trained with someone the director either knows personally or by reputation and that can be helpful, especially if your coach is well respected.

Special Skills

OK, the next section of your résumé is *special skills.*
Do you skateboard? Rock climb? Play the guitar? All of these are of interest to a casting director. Include them, but only if you really do what you claim.

Aha Moment!

Always tell the truth.
Don't lie. Don't ever lie. It's beneath you. And in the end it won't help. So be honest. Any director worth their salt will respect that.

Union Affiliations

Next up on the résumé is your *union affiliations.*

Just like autoworkers and grocery store clerks, actors have unions. There's the Screen Actor's Guild. This is for actors in movies and TV. There's Equity. This is for stage actors. There's AFTRA (American Federation of Television and Radio Actors). And there's the Extra's Union. You have to pay a fee to join any of these unions. For Equity and SAG, you have to have experience and be invited to join plus pay a fee.

Sometimes, the director needs an actor from a particular union, nothing you can do about that. Remember, *getting cast has nothing and everything to do with you.*

One final note about résumés: make sure it's typed neatly, no typos. Your picture and résumé are your calling card and you want to make a good impression.

Preparing for the Reading

You've handed over your headshot and résumé to the person receiving them. Please remember the person who takes the paperwork is as important a person as everybody else. Say "hello." And please and thank you.

It's time now to prep for the actual reading. You do this by finding a quiet place and studying your sides.

Sides

So, what is a side, you ask? Good question. I'm glad you asked, oh wise one. A *side* is a section of the script. It's the scene you will be auditioning with. Sometimes it will give you a character description, many times it won't.

You can be asked to read the side *cold*. That means you've never seen it before and you will read it "cold." Or you can be asked to read the side *prepared;* you got your sides a couple of days ago and you've had some time to prepare. With prepared auditions, especially in TV and film, memorize your lines. Do not, I repeat, do not come in and read off the paper. It's terribly bad form and makes it difficult to catch your face on camera.

Reading Tips

1. *Find the intention of your character.* Every character has something they must do. It could be to woo the girl, kill the beast, fight the evil bank robber, break up, run away. It's up to you, the actor, to figure out what is that intention. To find the intention, go to the script.

2. *Figure out why that's your intention.* Remember our earlier game of "How do you feel and why?" It will help you loads here because why you made that choice is as important as the choice. Let's say your character wants to break up with the girl in the scene. Why you want to break up with the girl will help you choose which emotion to play.

Let's do some examples. You want to break up with her because she cheated on you. You'd be mad, right? But if you wanted to break up with the girl because you're afraid of commitment, you'd be distant and cool. You see. You need to know why you're making the choices you make to understand which emotion to play.

Again, to find the why, look to the script for answers. However, if you can't find a clear reason why, make one up. It's better to be 100 percent wrong than 10 percent right.

3. *Make a choice and commit to it.*

Aha Moment!

Go all or go home.

Make a choice, my darling, and go with it. One hundred percent commit to whatever it is. The only way you can make a fool of yourself is to be afraid of making a fool of yourself. So once you've chosen, don't look back. No retreat. No surrender.

4. *Use what you know.* Back to that "being you" stuff. You've decided that your intention is to break up with the girl because she cheated on you and you're heartbroken. Great. Now go to your own life to make it real. If you've been cheated on in the past, I'm so sorry, but you can totally use that here. Play whatever emotion you had. Easy.

But what if you weren't cheated on in the past. Every relationship you've had has worked out. Wow for you, but as an actor, yikes, you're going to have to use memories of something similar. Was there a time your best friend hung out with someone other than you? Or your pet cat preferred the lap of a stranger? How did that feel? Now use that feeling to make it real.

5. *Show it.* You're not just a voice. You're also a body. What can you do with your body that will help manifest your intention? Back to that cheating girlfriend, the one you want to break up with. What can you do physically to build that intention? If onstage, you can walk off stage — that's a risky choice but memorable. If you're on camera, you can turn away, you can glare at her, you can laugh. Whatever choice you make, it must be true. Do not fake it. Directors know. It's our super power to sniff out untrue performances and destroy them.

In the Room

So, dear one, you've given your picture and résumé to the proper people. You've read over your side and you've figured out what your intention is and why. It's now time (dum de dum dum) to audition. But you got this under control 'cause you know *getting cast has nothing and everything to do with you.* But you still want to do a great job. Here's what you can expect when you step up to read ...

• Your heart will be racing like a jackhammer and your knees might be shaking. Cool! That's nerves. Use them.

• The director or casting director will ask you a few questions about yourself. Oftentimes that question is something like, "Tell me about yourself." This is where all that time you've spent learning about you pays off, because now you have lots to share. You can talk about what you like, what you don't like, your hobbies, how you feel about school, family, TV shows. You can chat about your dog Waiter (wait, that's my dog) or your Yu-Gi-Oh collection or cheerleading. The director wants to know about you. So talk. Oh, and don't be afraid to ask a question or two back — everyone likes to talk about themselves, including directors.

- You will then be asked to read. Commit fully to your choices. Remember, go all or go home.
- The director will either ask you to read more or not. It means absolutely nothing if they don't ask you to read on, so don't worry.
- The director will say, "thank you." You say, "thank you," too.
- You leave.

A Few Final Interview Tips Here

1. *Sit up straight.* I know that sounds like something your mother would say, but sometimes Mom is right.
2. *Answer with more than a single word.* If the casting director asks, "How are you?" Don't say "fine," and let it drop like a big old lead balloon. Say, "I'm good. How about you?" or "I'm great. Excited to be here. This is an awesome part, because ... " In other words, answer the question and then offer a bit more information.
3. *If you ask the person a question, listen to their answer.* Don't look away or at your shoes. Make eye contact. Show interest. Everyone has an interesting story to tell.

 **GOLD STAR**

For giving an incredible audition. Yay for you! Go to the back of the book, color a star. Any color you like. It's your star.

Stage Auditions

Stage auditions are interesting, because you can end up reading for just the director, or you can read for everyone. If you're lucky enough to have auditions in front of other actors, take advantage of this awesome opportunity by watching what the other actors do. Ask yourself, "Did I like that reading? Why or why not? What can I do different?"

Audition Mistakes

Oh my, how many young actors eliminate themselves from getting cast without saying a word? I have seen actors read books, text, and talk while other actors audition. Once, a kid actually fell asleep and started snoring. I kid you not. I have had actors tell me that they needed their karaoke CD louder so we couldn't hear their voice when they sang. Actors have argued with me, told me, the writer, they knew more about the character than I did. You know, it's almost like they want to *not* be cast. So for your reading pleasure, I've compiled a list!

Ten Things You Can Do to Give a Really Horrible Audition

1. *Move around a lot.* This is a goody — move about the stage because you think walking somehow implies intensity. Or meander aimlessly, wandering from one side of the stage to the other until the director is dizzy. Oh, and shuffle your feet. Directors don't want to hear the dialogue anyway.

2. *Mumble like you got marbles in your mouth.* Yes, speak so quietly the director can't hear, or run the words together so the director has no idea what you're saying. Perhaps the director will cast you just to avoid the ensuing headache you're giving him?

3. *Never ever look at your partner.* Keep your head buried in the script so the director can't see your face. Why would a director want to see your expressions when she can have a wonderful view of the back of a piece of paper?

4. *Don't ask for pronunciation of words.* Giggle and stumble over the dialogue some poor writer has spent hours, and sometimes years, laboring over. Oh, and bonus points if you can combine this with meandering across the floor. It will create quite a concerto of awful.

5. *Come unprepared.* What better way to be memorable than making the director really angry by being late or not knowing what you're reading or not having a pencil?

6. *When you have found a way to read, stick with it.* Yes. Come in to the audition convinced you have found the perfect approach. It doesn't matter that the director asks you to read it differently, just keep doing it the same way.

7. *Take lots and lots of unnecessary pauses.* All those tedious pauses will not only make the director think you're deep and thoughtful, it will put the director to sleep and who doesn't need a good rest during auditions?

8. *Don't bother with manners.* Barrel in, talk about yourself ad nauseam, read and then leave, never taking a moment to say thank you. Your time is so much more valuable than the director's.

9. *Don't listen to the director.* Let me give you an example. I had a group of young actors who were "trained." Heaven help us. And their coach had told them that whenever they audition to make sure to say their name and what they'd be singing before they sang.

   Now this could have been nice if they had been singing for the first time and I didn't know who these kids were, but I knew these actors well and I had said not five minutes before, "I'm in a hurry.

We have a lot to do so let's speed through this." They apparently thought the request wasn't for them. 'Cause every time one of those "trained" actors got up to sing, I heard their name and what they were singing. Every time. So do exactly as you've been told to, even if the director has pleaded with you to do things different. This makes quite the impression.

10. *Choose completely inappropriate material.* Play an eighty-year-old woman with ten kids from the Appalachian Mountains if you're a guy or an aging rich widow or a dad of seven if you're fourteen. There's nothing more a director wants to see than a twelve-year-old girl singing "Let Me Entertain You," from *Sweet Charity.* Directors love feeling uncomfortable or having their time wasted with your reading of something you'd never in a million years be right for.

Uhm, thanks for listening. Now that I got that out of my system, let's try this again. Let me give you some final tips to give a really killer audition. May I present to you, oh brilliant thespian ...

Ten Rules of a Great Audition

1. *I will not move, unless there is a clear intention behind it.* Even if I have to staple my feet to the floor.
2. *I will speak clearly.*
3. *I will make eye contact.*
4. *I will ask how to pronounce words. In fact, if I have any kind of question about my part, I will ask!* Because I know the director is as eager as I to do a great job. Sometimes you won't understand the director's answer. That's OK. Ask the director to explain. And if you still don't understand what she's asking for, that's also OK, so just try something — anything. Stand on a chair. Giggle. Whatever comes to your mind. It's better to be one hundred percent wrong than a little right.
5. *I will be on time and prepared.* If you can get a copy of the script ahead of time, awesome — read it. Always bring a pencil and a pen. Have your headshot ready to offer should the director need it. And it couldn't hurt to have a pad of paper, however small. You never know when you'll need to take a note or give someone a phone number.

Trivia

When they were casting *The Last of the Finest*, Joe Pantaliono — lovingly known as Joey Pants — came in to audition ... with a briefcase. Not filled with scripts or even cookies for the director, but wigs. Yes, his case was filled with toupees. You see, Joe is bald, but sometimes directors like him to have hair. So he had hair. Boy did he have hair. Somewhat bald, more hair but still bald, full head of hair — Joey P was ready. He got the role!

6. *I will not be afraid to take a risk.* Auditioning is like a dance. The director is looking to see if she can lead and you can follow. There has been many a time I have cast because I saw growth and change in an actor during audition.

Take Bobby MC for example. Bobby was a young actor who came to us a few years back. Tall, gawky, with a radio announcer's deep baritone, Bobby wasn't what we were thinking we wanted for the part. And in truth, he wasn't the most polished actor, the most graceful dancer, or the most rangeful singer. But he was willing to take risks. Man oh man he put it all out there, trying whatever we asked him to do and sometimes offering his own spin. He got the role, 'cause we knew he'd give it his all and he'd be fun to work with, not because he was necessarily right.

7. *I will quit with the pauses already.* Pauses don't make a director think you're deep; they make a director bored. If you can't make those emotional transitions fast, don't make them. Find another way to go.

8. *I will take a moment to say thanks.* And please. Please and thank you are such nice words and so underused. As are thank you notes. Write one to the director. It will mean something.

9. *I will listen to the director and adjust accordingly.*

10. *I will choose material right for me.* You're you. Embrace it. Sing it from the mountaintops. And find audition pieces for parts that you might play.

Here are a few wonderful examples:

Ordinary People
Little Women
Anne of Green Gables
Romeo and Juliet
Twelfth Night

And any Totally Teen Show that Showdown has written:
Bard High
Usher
Gumshoe High
Quixote
Jeckyl and Hydes

One Final Thought ... or Seven

Odds are it will take twenty auditions for you to get a callback. Twenty. It's a numbers game. And the more time you can put your best foot out there, the better your chances of scoring that part. Keep at it!

Dress for success. This means that when you go to the audition, whisper your character's look, don't shout it. So let's say you're up for the part of Dorothy in *The Wizard of OZ*. Don't wear a gingham dress with a white blouse and red shoes. But you could maybe wear a skirt with a plain top and pull your hair back. Make sense? If you overdo it, you could alienate the director. I mean, what if he's doing a hip, Goth version of *The Wizard of OZ?* Your country girl would throw him off.

You will not get cast for a bazillion reasons. Most of those reasons having little to do with you. Here's one from my rejection book:

When we were trying to get our play *Very Moliery* published, we were told by the publisher, who was interested, he wanted to wait to see how another one of our shows did with them. The other show? ... It was completely different.

Remember ... *getting cast has nothing and everything to do with you!*

43

Chapter Five

You Got the Part!

Trivia
Daniel Radcliffe, the actor who plays Harry Potter, originally didn't want the part of Harry. In fact, he hadn't even read the book. Daniel's passion at the time he got cast was the WWF (World Wrestling Federation). Wonder what would have happened had he not auditioned, would he be a big time wrestler now?

The director loved you. He thought you were amazing, you got cast. Of course, look at who you are and what an awesome job you did. First, please accept this …

Silver Latte

It's time to celebrate. Treat yourself to something delish. May I suggest a light mocha frap from Starbucks or a Cold Stone Creamery super sundae?

OK, tummy happy? Heart singing? It's time to get to work. But which work?

Film Vs. Television Vs. Stage
Though you might act in each medium — TV, stage, and movie — the performance you will give will be very different and yet incredibly similar. Confusing, huh? No! You've got this handy dandy book, which will explain it all for you.

Film
Let's start with *film acting*.

In many ways, film and TV drama are very similar. Both film and TV drama require you to give an internal performance. This means that all your gut-wrenching emotions are under the surface. In other words, you're feeling it, but you're not emoting it. Does this make sense? In this type of work, the camera is in close. It's like the audience is two inches from your face. And if you're too expressive, you'll look like a clown, so you have to hold back and let the camera do the work.

How about an example? In the movie *The Bourne Ultimatum*, Julia Styles gives this wonderful performance. She's talking to Matt Damon who is asking her why she's helping him. For a good fifteen seconds, she says nothing, yet the expression in her face says mouthfuls, but still she is very subtle, because her performance is in her eyes. Finally, she says, "It was hard for me." Wow, huh? Ironically enough, she didn't need to speak because her face said everything. She could have said nothing and we would have known that it was hard for her.

However, the amount of pauses Julia took plus the subtlety of her performance would be lost on a stage. And worse yet, it would be really boring. Do you now begin to see how TV drama and sitcom and stage performance is different?

In addition, film acting relies heavily on technique or the ability to repeat a performance over and over again. With film, the same scene is run many times because the director: may not get the performance he needs from one of the actors; needs to get the Master shot (that's a big wide shot that has everybody in it); isn't happy with the lighting or the sound; needs differing POV shots (those are over-the-shoulder shots); may want lots of close-ups. It's the actor's job to recreate the same performance each time. And often the actor has to do this lickity-split.

However, one of the easier things about acting for the camera is you don't have to worry about pacing or picking up your cues. That's done in editing. And aside from hitting your mark, or being where you're supposed to be when you're supposed to be there, it's not your job to concern yourself with where the camera is. That's the director's headache. However, the more you know about camera angles, the more an asset you'll be when the director is framing a shot.

Trivia

During the filming of *Jurassic Park*, Steven Spielberg was framing a shot for Richard Attenborough. Richard, a world-class director himself, saw what Steven was doing, knew that he wasn't in frame, and scooted over. Steven was thrilled to be working with someone who knew how the camera worked.

Sitcom Acting

Sitcom acting is a cross between film and stage. You need to be bigger and broader than you do in film and TV drama, but you're still working in front of a camera, which is no longer inches, but a foot or two away from you.

45

Many sitcoms use a three-camera approach, which is three different cameras on three different parts of the stage operated by three different cameramen, but guided by one director. The reason for the three cameras is to save money. And time. With three cameras going at once, the director is getting full coverage (lots of shots) and can then choose the final cut in editing.

Trivia
Desi Arnez, Lucille Ball's husband, was the producer for the *I Love Lucy* Show. Desi created the three-camera technique because he thought Lucy was so funny he wanted to make sure the audience didn't miss a moment of her performance.

Sitcom production is organized much like a play. On Monday, actors and crew sit around a table and read the show. Changes in the script are made throughout the rehearsal process, which is usually Monday to Friday. On Friday night the show is taped before a live audience. The audience's live laughter will be used to sweeten the already existing laugh track.

Theatre Acting
This type of acting is the biggest and broadest because an actor's performance might have to reach someone 100 rows back as well as twenty feet from the stage. We'll get into some tips of how to give a kick-butt theatre performance later on, but for now, we know that acting for the stage is bigger and broader.

First Rehearsal

From the Director's POV
The first rehearsal is nerve-racking. For me, this is when my stomach is all butterfly-y. I'm excited. Nervous. Uncertain. A million thoughts run through my head. Did I do a good job casting? Will the actors like their roles? Will I know what to do with the show? Will we be ready by opening night? Will the actors like me? Will I be able to communicate what I want? Aaaach. This is when I need a hug.

Reassuring isn't it to know that most directors are as nervous as you? And they want to do an amazing job too. They just won't show it. They can't. The team needs a leader, not a nervous wreck. Plus the director must be five steps ahead to keep the show on schedule; there's no time for insecurity.

From the Actor's POV

This is the first time you will meet everyone and probably the last time you will see the show in its entirety before dress rehearsals.

"There is no way I'm going to get the part if I'm up against her!"
— Emma Watson,
who did get the part of Hermione in the Harry Potter movies

The Table Read

Most stage shows begin with the table read. Everybody is gathered in some kind of assemblage to listen to the script being read. Many young actors make huge mistakes at this juncture, frustrating the director and crew and they don't even know it. Let me enlighten you, grasshoppa ...

How an Actor Should Behave at a Table Read

1. The *actor* has a sharpened pencil, sometimes two or seven in case someone forgot theirs. The *actor* has her script. And from here on, always comes to rehearsal with a pencil and script.
2. Cell phones, pagers, and any kind of poddy devices are turned off. And the *actor* never ever checks his techno-toys while the reading is going on. That's what breaks are for.
3. To the best of the *actor's* ability, she gives a performance-level reading. No holding back and waiting to get the show up on its feet. The *actor* commits fully at this level so the director knows she made a great choice in casting and knows what she has to work with.
4. The *actor* listens attentively at the reading. The *actor* doesn't talk to other actors or get up and go to the bathroom. The *actor* respects everyone's work.
5. When the director asks if there are any questions, the *actor* asks, knowing that whatever he is curious about, probably the rest of the company will want to know as well. And vice versa, when another actor asks a question, the *actor* listens so the answer doesn't have to be repeated.

That's it. Pretty simple stuff, huh? Yet you'd be surprised how many actors don't do this. They text during a reading, they talk to other actors, and they don't listen when someone else is asking a question.

Most directors have eagle eyes. We see everything. It's another of our super powers. And we store that information in our high-powered memory banks for future shows determining if we want to work with you again.

Jacob J is a prime example. Ah, JJ. This young spud came to us at the ripe old age of twelve. A wiry snip of a boy, in JJ's own words, "I was really obnoxious." (We didn't think so). Anyway, JJ grew up into a handsome, confident sixteen-year-old young man and was given a decent-sized role. This is always a concern for us, because when dealing with young actor companies, how a lead behaves off stage is very important. Young actors model their behavior after whoever is leading. JJ rose to the occasion and more. He was responsible. Kind. Respectful. He set the bar and everyone followed right in behind. Because of his behavior, we happily cast him in a starring role.

Getting the Show on Its Feet

The table read is done. It's time to begin rehearsals. What can you expect? Well, first, rehearsals may or may not be onstage at this juncture. Rehearsals can be in a rehearsal hall, or office, or someone's living room. And you'll be given a rehearsal schedule so you can know where you're supposed to be and when.

Usually at the first rehearsal the director will talk. A lot. The director may talk about his approach or what he wants from the characters or how the set will look. It's rare that a director will jump right in and start blocking, but some may — depends on the director.

And though every director has their own style of working, most directors use similar terminology, which is why I have compiled a vocabulary list. But don't worry, I won't test you on this at the end of the chapter.

Vocabulary

Stage directions are the movements you make on a stage. Stage directions are a bit complicated. So don't sweat it if at first you don't understand. You'll get them.

Stage directions are given in two ways. *Actor's direction* is from the actor's POV looking out at the audience. *Director's direction* is from the director's POV looking at you, the actor. Said another way, you're the actor and you're looking out at the audience, your left is going to be different than the director's left. The director's left is your right. Understand? When the director says move left, he means his left. Which is your right. And when he says stage left, he means your left. So stage left is actors' left. Left is director's left (your right). Got it so far? Great. Let's move on to moving *upstage* and *downstage*.

Trivia

In the early days, stages were raked. That means the stage was at an angle so that the audience could see. The rear part of the stage was raked up while the front part of the stage near the audience was titled down. Hence we use the terms upstage and downstage today.

When a director tells you to move upstage, he is saying move towards the back wall, away from the audience. When he tells you to move downstage, you move towards the audience. Moving *center stage,* you go to the center of the stage.

OK, got all that? Good. Move downstage, actor's left. Which way do you go? You move towards the director to your left. Move upstage right. You move away from the director to your right.

But we're not done yet, 'cause there are different stage shapes:

Proscenium: Usually a raised stage, the audience directly faces the stage. Think traditional theatres and you know what I mean.

Horseshoe: The audience is on three sides of the stage. It looks pretty much as it sounds. The audience is in a horseshoe shape around the stage.

In the Round: The audience completely surrounds the stage on all four sides.

Black Box: It is probably as you picture it. The theatre is a big black box and the audience can be anywhere the director wishes.

So, you're in a Black Box theatre and the director says, "Move downstage left." Now what do you do? The director is always your audience so take direction from where she sits.

My last and final words about stage directions: *write them down!* I promise you will not remember them, so write them down. You can come up with your own code system as to where you're supposed to be and how you're supposed to move. I've seen squiggly lines, long ponderous sentences, and stick figures. *Do not,* I repeat, *do not,* trust your memory. As sure as shootin' you will forget and make the director very cranky. *Write it down!*

All that said, let's go on with the vocabulary lesson:

Cue: The line before your line. A cue is what is said prior to the line you are going to say. When learning your lines, it's a really good idea to know your cues as well. In fact, may I suggest that you highlight both your lines and your cues in your script?

Cheat out: Turning your body towards the audience. Almost always it is expected that you will cheat out, which is turning your body as much towards the audience as is realistic, but your face towards the person you are speaking to.

Upstaging: Turning your body away from the audience. There are three different ways that upstaging is used. *Upstaging yourself* is allowing another actor to block the audience's vision of you. Usually he is standing upstage of you and you are turned away from the audience. *Upstaging someone else* is placing yourself upstage of your partner and the audience cannot see his face. To *move upstage* is to move away from the audience.

Project: Speaking loud enough for the audience to hear you. Sometimes this is called using your outdoor voice. But projecting is not shouting. It's speaking loudly from your diaphragm so the audience can hear you.

Taking Focus: Doing a distracting movement. None of us is the center of the universe. Theatre is an ensemble. When you are onstage and not speaking, it's up to you to support the other actors who are talking. You do this by being in character. The problem many actors make is that they think the bigger the gesture, the more they are in character. No. The larger their movements, the more they are taking focus. When you are not speaking but onstage and not part of the scene, keep gestures to a minimum.

Dropping a Line: Forgetting your lines.

Cue Pick Up: Cutting down the length of time between your line and another's. Many actors believe that cue pick up is speaking faster. It isn't. It means cutting out those interminable pauses between your line and the previous actor's line.

Notes: Comments from the director or directors. These are the pearls of wisdom the director has for you to improve your performance. I can tell you a couple of things about this. When the director speaks, *listen!* Some directors have no idea what they're doing. They seem to be incoherent blobs who are totally clueless as to what makes a good show. You must listen to them too. Do your best to give them what they want, then go home, drink lots of milkshakes, and cry into your pillow. Never work with them again. Regardless, when a director talks, *write it down!* Literally. Whatever the director tells you to do, write it down.

Crew: The backstage dudes and dudettes. It's helpful to know who they be and what jobs they do. Crew vocabulary is not to be confused with the words crew say. Although, they could say some of the vocabulary you've just learned. The crew vocabulary in this chapter is for you to learn the jobs that are in a crew and what those jobs entail.

A *stage manager* is the second in command to the director. The stage manager runs the show when the director is not around. The stage manager takes copious staging notes. Mr. Stage Manager also can: run backstage when the show is up and running, be the director when the director is no longer with the show, oversee all the crews to make sure they are meeting deadlines, and oversee actors to make sure they are on time.

The *producer* is the head administrator, the Big Cheese, and often the money person. The producer is often depicted with a cigar in his mouth, shouting about money and time — that's not that far from the truth. Except sometimes the producer is a woman and smoking is really uncool these days, but you get the picture. The producer in Broadway theatre got the funding for the show and is now making sure everything and everyone including the director is doing their job. In local theatre, the producer can be the harried lunatic running around doing a bazillion jobs or is responsible for ticket sales, depending on what's needed. In film, the producer has brought all the talent together. In TV, the producer is usually a writer. And don't get me started on supervising producers and assistant producers — it's crazy, man, crazy!

The *choreographer* is the director of the dance numbers. This person is responsible for any numbers that require dance. Sometimes the director will do simple musical staging, but most times, if there's music and movement, there's the choreographer.

The *musical director* is the director of music. If there's a song to be sung, the MD will teach it to you. If there's a tune in your heart, the director of music will find the harmony and make you learn it. Interim music, preshow tunes, if it's got a beat, the musical director oversees it.

The *chain of command* is the order for who to report to. If there's a problem or a question, you need to know who to go to. The chain of command works like this: the producer makes sure there are butts in the seats and reports to the director; the stage manager makes sure that the crew is working well and that actors are behaving and reports to the director; the director oversees the look and sound of the entire production and reports to the producer, sort of. Some directors think they are God and report to no one. Foolish mortals. The choreographer, who is sometimes the director, reports to the director. The music director reports to the director.

What this means is when you are receiving notes, you will only receive notes directly from the director if it has to do with your acting or overall performance. If there's a problem with your dancing, the director will go to the choreographer and tell him, the choreographer will then tell you. The same is true with musical directors. If the director likes your singing, he won't tell you, the musical director will.

It's a cumbersome system that often seems to waste time to me. Why can't I just go over and talk to that person directly? Because it's disrespectful. The music director may not agree with the director's note and they will need to discuss it before giving it to the actor.

The *dance captain* is the choreographer's assistant. This loverly human knows all the dance steps inside and out and will teach them to you and review them when you forget.

The *accompanist* is the piano player who plays during rehearsal. Sometimes this eighty-eight key'd Jack will play during the show. He could also be the music director.

Clearly a lot of people can go into making up a show. In fact, there's many more than this. Wardrobe, lighting, props, house manager, but you don't really need to know them at this stage of the show. Ha! Get it? "Stage" of the show. See? 'Cause you're an actor and you're onstage now. I think it's time for ...

It's time to kick back and notice what all you've learned. Whoa. Treat yourself to something delish. How's about a Krispy Kreme donut or a BBQ chicken salad from California Pizza Kitchen?

Chapter Six

Cindy's Approach to a Role

Check In

Before we go any further, it's time to check in.

So, how ya feelin'? Excited? Overwhelmed? Confused? Educated? You're doin' great. It's a lot to take in. And you don't have to do it all at once. It's OK to put the book down for a while. Have some fun. In fact, why don't we play a game or two?

Games

1. Draw a picture of you receiving your Tony (for theatre excellence) or Oscar (film excellence) or Emmy (TV excellence) or all three.
2. Write your acceptance speech for your AFI (American Film Institute) Lifetime Achievement Award.
3. Go to the 99 Cent Store and buy a coloring book and a box of crayons. Go home, put on your favorite music, and color away, baby.
4. Make a hot fudge sundae with extra whip cream. Dive in.
5. Go to the library and check out five movies. You can go genre: check out all action pics or comedies or sci-fi thrillers. You can be an eclectic person: take out an animated film, a romance, a foreign film, a medical drama, and a classic. Treat yourself to popcorn, your favorite kind of movie candy, and a soda. Go home and watch all the movies in one day. Invite a friend.

Oh my, that feels so much better. It's important to remind ourselves to have fun. Being an actor is neat. In what other profession do you get to play make-believe?

OK, back to the salt mines, or the stage as the case may be.

Creating the Role

You are now deep in rehearsal land and it's time to create a memorable character. Which way to go? Which way to go? There are as many approaches to creating a character as there are actors. Here are just a few approaches:

1. *Out to In:* start with physical mannerisms and build your character from there.

2. *Research:* a lot of writing here with biographies and such.
3. *The Method:* actually living like the character as much as possible.
4. *Instinctive:* Throw a lot out to the director and see what she likes.

Aha Moment!

There is no right way to approach a role.

You need to find what works for you. It may be a combination of a bunch of different philosophies or the complete immersion into one learning style. There are lots of coaches out there who will tell you, "It's my way or the highway." They believe that only they have the answers. To them I say, "Poppycosh!" They are afraid that if you try another's approach you'll like it better and they'll be out of a job. Try different teachers! When you feel like you've learned what you can, move on to the next coach until you find the path that you like. Life is about living, trying things, learning. Embrace that. Cherish it.

Over the next few chapters I'm going to offer up a few different styles from different directors that I dearly respect. My suggestion is you try out each approach. Take what works for you and lose what doesn't. Remember, this is about learning who you are, discovering what you like, what matters, and what's important to you. The more you know about yourself, the more you can bring to the role.

How Cindy Approaches a Role

I wish I had a way cool name for my approach, like (ahem) The Hyde Definitive Approach to Acting and All Things Purple. But I don't. Sad face. I think that's because my approach to acting is a mixture of many differing styles with an emphasis on performance. Said another way: you've been cast, you have a job to do, so my approach focuses on getting you to performance level as quickly as possible.

My approach is layered. I work like a painter, I shade as I go. Does this make sense? Creating a character cannot happen all at once. The character has to be built step by step. Bit by bit. Rome wasn't built in a day, and neither can a living three-dimensional human being.

Let's walk through my steps in brief then in detail.

In *step one,* you answer four questions:

1. Who is your character?
2. What is your character's intention?
3. Where is your character coming from?
4. How does your character feel about the other characters?

Once you have answered these questions, you go to *step two:* find out how your character feels and why.

Gosh, I can't emphasize that enough. How does your character feel and why? And you must know her feelings in your core. Does that make sense? Knowing how a character feels vs. understanding how he feels is the difference between being empathetic and sympathetic. Sympathy is merely understanding, but empathy is actually having walked in another's moccasins and slept in their bed. OK, enough with the metaphors and on to *step three* of Cindy's Approach to Acting: let go.

The final step is the hardest and most confusing because I want you to let everything you've done go. Simply listen and react. That's it. Just listen and react. Some coaches call this living in the moment. Others call it keeping everything fresh. It's acting as if you the character have never been on this journey before.

Oh, one final note, these steps don't necessarily happen in order. You might go from step one to step three or you might hit a few questions in step one, jump to step three, back to step two. Acting is supposed to be fluid, but since this book isn't meant to be flowy, we're going to review my steps in step order.

Step One: The Questions
1. Who Is Your Character?

The answer to this question lies within the script. Whatever you need to know about your character, whether implied or direct, lies between the pages. Some actors write lengthy bios to uncover their character. I'm not really big on those. Honestly, I find them a waste of time, unless, and this is a big unless, the bio information comes from the script and is necessary to the character right now, then it's totally valuable. Let's go back to *The Sound of Music* example and review just a few bobs and bits of what we learned in chapter three about Maria:

- She's from Austria.
- She's an orphan.
- It's the 1930s.
- She loves the Alps.
- She was raised by nuns.

Your purpose in writing a bio is not to serve your imagination, but to serve the show and ultimately the audience. Your character bio along with every other bit of work you will do is to help you give a truer performance for the audience.

So let's begin with *she's from Austria*. Well, what is Austria? Can you find it on a map? Go ahead, look, I'll wait. What did you find out? It's a small country near Germany. OK. But knowing that, does that help us create a more real character? Hmmmm. Let's think this through.

At the end of the story Maria must escape from the Nazis through the hills of Austria. And she's not just saving her own hide, she's saving the lives of her children and husband, so unless Maria cares little for them and is willing to get them captured, she better know for certain how to get out of Austria. So, knowing the geography of Austria is necessary to create a real character. In fact, I think the actress playing Maria better know more than just Austria is a small country next to Germany. She would need to know which hills Maria is referring to and what they look like. Where is the convent in relation to the hills?

Is there anything else we might need to know about Austria? Austrians have a very definite culture. They dress a certain way and that style of dressing leads to a certain way of walking. Think about it. A woman who walks in heels walks differently than a woman walking in tennis shoes. So playing Maria, you'd need to learn a bit about Austrian culture. But not today's culture, the culture of the 1930s when the play took place because it's relevant to the performance.

Austrians speak with an accent, at least to we Americans. Well, an accent could be nice, but does that really serve the character? Asked another way, is the accent necessary for the audience to understand Maria's character? I don't think so. What do you think?

Anything more we need to know about Austria?

Since *The Sound of Music* is also about the takeover of Austria, it could be good to know about their politics. But not today's political system, because that's not relevant to Maria's character — the political system when the story took place is relevant.

Anything else? Maybe. Maybe not. It's up to you. And the only way to learn what questions matter for your performance is to do bios. The more bios you do over your career, the more you will learn what questions to ask yourself. You will learn by doing. Eventually, you'll figure out what works for you.

Let's try building a bio for another character from another show. *Grease* is the infamous 50s musical. Who doesn't know *Grease*? Throw a stone and it will hit some school that's done the show. OK, so what about the character of Danny Zuko, the hero and leader of the T-Birds who falls in love with Sandy. Let's look at a few facts we can find in the script:

- He goes to Rydell High School.
- It's 1959.
- Over the holiday he dated a girl named Sandy.
- He belongs to the T-Birds.

Let's start with *he goes to Rydell High School.* Where is Rydell and does it matter? Is it in the Midwest, the South, or New York? With a little bit of digging on the Internet, I found out that Rydell High School is loosely based on William Howard Taft School in Chicago. Does that help build the character of Danny? It could. High school in Chicago is very different than high school in a small town. How is it different? Kids from the city are more sophisticated because they're exposed to cutting edge culture, yet they are more guarded because they need to protect themselves from crime. That tells us that Danny probably has a few walls, not an open kind of character. Anything else we need to know about Rydell? Is it a big school or a small school? That could affect how Danny relates to kids. A big school means he's, again, more guarded. In a small school everyone knows everyone. Hmmmm. As an actor you will need to decide which is best.

Next bit of script information is *the play is set in 1959.* Well, what was life like in the public schools of Chicago in 1959? Were there cliques like there are now? Yes. There were the Pink Ladies and the T-Birds. But were there more? Did people from one group hang out with people from another? If they didn't, then Danny being willing to hang out with the jocks for Sandy says a whole lot about his feelings for her, doesn't it? He's willing to risk being an outcast of his group for her.

Bit by bit, bird by bird, you will take the information given to you by the playwright and decide what you need to investigate. It's your character, the choice is yours. And if you find yourself wondering, "What do I ask next?" ask yourself, "Self, what do I still not understand about my character? What do I still not know?"

2. What Is Your Character's Intention?

Now you have some idea of who you are playing, it's time to decide what she wants. Again, you go back to the script.

Characters generally have three kinds of wants. They have an *overall want,* which is their drive throughout the play; it is what motivates them to journey the story. Characters also have *scene-by-scene wants.* These are specific goals within each scene to help them achieve their overall want. Finally, characters have an *inner want,* or emotional need. It is usually something they must learn about themselves and its unknown to them until the end of the show.

For example, I want to get this book published. That's my big overall want. I'm writing a chapter right now, so my scene want is to get me closer to my overall goal. But I don't know what my emotional need is to publish this book. Perhaps it's because I have a need for recognition or approval or respect. I guess I'll find that out once I get the book published.

Every character, no matter how small, in every scene has an overall intention, a scene-by-scene intention, and an inner yearning. Intentions can change, but your character must have intention at all times.

Back to Danny Zuko from *Grease*. What is his overall intention? To win Sandy's heart. What does he do scene by scene to achieve that intention? Well, he tries to be the kind of guy he thinks Sandy wants. He tries to play it cool. He pretends she doesn't matter to him. Eventually he realizes that he has to be himself.

In *Legally Blonde,* Elle wants to win the heart of her college sweetheart. She does this by going to Harvard Law School. Trying to get into his classes. Interning at the same firm. Finally, she realizes that he isn't who she thought he was and what really counts in life is being true to herself.

Hmmmm, seems a lot of characters learn that it's important to trust themselves. Not sure what I think about that. What do you think?

3. Where Is Your Character Coming From?

Many actors mistakenly believe that their performance begins onstage. So they don't get into character until they are literally standing in front of the audience. Oh my, this is wrong — so wrong. You see, it is the actor's job to create an alternate reality for the audience. And the actor can't do that if they get into character onstage. That's way too late. To create a believable performance, actors must enter the stage in character, as if the character's world had been happening simultaneously, like an alternate reality that has always coexisted. Does this make sense? Foolishly, actors also drop their character after they leave the stage. You don't come in and out of your reality, do you? No. And neither should your character. Once the journey of the story begins, your character is fully involved until she's achieved her goal.

How do you maintain a character? Before every single scene in the show, you must know where your character is and where they are headed. Did he come from the park or school or a fight with his ex-girlfriend? Is he late? Is he on time? Was he in a conversation and with whom? Was the conversation going as planned or did it get off somehow? Was he alone? Where you came from and what happened while your character's there affects how you enter the scene and the actions you will take within the scene.

Trivia

Uta Hagen, legendary actress and acting coach, was doing a show in New York. Her character was supposed to enter the second act having just come from a dinner party. But no matter how Uta tried, she could not find the rhythms and the voice of her character in the second act. It seemed ridiculous that coming from a dinner party would matter that much to her performance. But it did. With no other option, she actually had a dinner catered backstage. Yep. During intermission she and her fellow actors dined on fine china and linen while chatting like their characters. It made all the difference in the world to her performance in the second act!

Let's talk about that Maria again. In the opening number she's flitting about the stage singing about living hills. She's having a grand old time until she realizes she's late for Mass. What if Maria were having a really crappy day when she entered the hills? What if she got yelled at and stubbed her toe and was hungry? Would she sing the same as if she'd had a good day? No. She'd be snapping that song and probably singing grumpily, doing her best to make herself feel better. OK, what if Maria had met the man of her dreams before she entered the hills? Would that affect the way she sang? Of course it would. She might forget her lyrics. She might sing dreamily. You see? What's happened to your character prior to entering each scene will affect how she enters.

Let's talk about another character. Lumiere in *Beauty and the Beast* sings to Belle that he wants her to be their guest. What if prior to coming on he heard the beast was moving to Africa and the curse would never be broken? Would he sing the song differently? You bet. He'd rush right through that puppy to get to the Beast so he could stop him.

Where your character came from and what happened while your character was there completely sets the tone for his behavior in the following scene. So you the actor must go through the script and figure out, before every scene, where was your character and what happened.

4. How Does Your Character Feel about the Other Characters?

As each of us is different, so is our relationship to each person we come in contact with. We feel differently about our mom, Aunt Susan, the guy who bags the groceries, and even the dog, Waiter. And because we feel differently about each person, we treat them differently. For example, if I'm mad at my son, I might lose my temper. But if I'm furious with my boss, I will keep my tone in check 'cause I don't want to get fired. I will hug my son in a way I might not hug my cousin. I have different feelings and histories with each person and I will accordingly treat them different. This is also true of your character. And it's up to you the actor to figure out what your emotional connections are to each of the other characters. Do you love them? Like them? Hate them? Envy them? What is your history with those characters? Have you known them a long time and shared your deepest darkest secrets or has your character known them for moments? All of this will affect how your character communicates with them.

Let's talk about Danny Zuko again. He's going to behave differently with Sandy than he is with Rizo. He's in love with Sandy. He might check his temper, he might smile more, certainly he'd flirt with Sandy, but Rizo is an old girlfriend. He doesn't care what she thinks of him so he will be more cavalier with her. Does this make sense?

This applies to every character your character comes in contact with. Your character must have a relationship to everyone onstage.

In addition, every noun your character utters must also have an emotional connotation. Try this for me — say the name of your best friend. Now say the name of your sibling. Now say "Mom." Now say the name of a hated teacher. Did you notice how your tone changed? It's the same thing for your character.

When Tevye sings of his beloved Anatefka, it's not just a word on a page to him. It's a feeling and a story and history. Anatefka is a piece of his soul as is his scary Aunt Tzeitel and Lazer Wolf the butcher. And the actor playing Tevye must feel those emotional connections whenever he says those names or it won't be real to the audience.

A Character Game

Purpose of the game:
Immerse yourself in your character's world.

Directions:
1. Go to the library and check the music CDs that you think your character would listen to.
2. Figure out the food your character would eat and the utensils they might use.
3. Pick out an outfit they would wear.
4. For an afternoon, eat the way they would eat, listen to their music, and dress the way they dress. Live the way your character would.

Step Two: How does the Character Feel and Why?

As we talked about your feelings and why in Chapter One, you must now do the same for your character. Over and over ask yourself, "How does my character feel about this? Why?"

- How does Maria feel about living in Austria? Why?
- How does Maria feel about being an orphan? Why?
- How does Maria feel about children? Why?

Why is it important to know how your character feels? Feelings are the guide into their heart. How your character feels tells you what matters to your character. And most important, knowing the feelings is the bridge to you. It is the ticket to you understanding the character. Does this make sense? You have never lived in Maria's Austria, but you know how it feels to love a place or a person or a thing so much that you would do anything for it. Do you see, my lovely? The way you connect with your character is through your feelings. It is empathy for your character. I think if each of us would take the time to empathize with another's feelings, we'd stop being so mad at each other. We'd stop being scared of each other. The world might feel like a safer place.

In Showdown, the theatre camp I help run for teens, we Circle Up whenever anyone has an issue or has something to share or needs to talk. We say, "Circle up!" and everyone joins the circle. *Everyone!* And like King Arthur and his knights, we sit in a circle so that everyone may be seen and nobody becomes more important than anybody else. In these circles we talk. But mostly we listen. We listen to the fears and joys and confusions of other campers. We listen, but we don't fix. We don't say, "It's gonna be OK," or "Don't feel that way," or even applaud those who share. We simply listen. We don't fix because we believe that everyone is OK no matter the feeling and there's nothing to fix. We don't fix because we need to just listen, and we don't fix because it gives us room to have our own feelings as we listen to the heart of someone else. Circling Up is so incredibly healing. And within the circle we have learned that everyone is the same as us underneath. Whether they are tall, leggy blondes or short, dark brunettes, in some fashion they have walked our walk and talked our talk.

Finding a Character's Feelings

To find a character's feelings, all you have to do is ask yourself, "How does my character feel about that? Why?" You want to know why they feel that way because it will tell you what action your character will take.

Let me show you what I mean. Let's look at Danny Zuko again. And let's use the scene where Danny is dissed by Sandy. How does he feel about that? Angry? Hurt? Confused? If he's angry, why is he angry? Is it because Sandy has done this to him before? Oh, then he might be guarded when he's with her. He doesn't want to get hurt again. If he thinks it's funny, why does he think it's funny that she dissed him? Maybe it's because he doesn't take her seriously. OK then, he might be cavalier in his reaction to her. Is he confused that she rejected him? Why? Because she said she loved him the night before. So he might not trust her now. Do you see? You need to know the feeling to make it real. You need to know why so you can figure out what next step your character will take.

But what if you don't know how your character feels? Or you know how he feels but you just don't get it. This is when you would go back to your life. Back to Mr. Zuko and let's say Sandy is rejecting Danny only this time the director says he wants Danny to be confused. But you don't get Danny being confused. You think any guy worth his salt would be angry as a mad hatter with Sandy. And you don't understand how Danny could feel this way. Ah, the actor's ancient dilemma: the director wants you to play something you don't agree with. Oh, my young actor friend, this is your job. You must do what the director asks you to do. So you have got to find it within yourself to make Danny confused, and make it real, whether you agree or not.

After berating the director silently and mumbling to the shower walls about how unfair it is that the director gets to do this — 'cause you have to get your resentment out or you will struggle with the task — it's time to find those feelings for the character. To do that, you've got to empathize with Danny Zuko. Ask yourself, "Was there ever a time in my life when I was confused instead of mad that someone rejected me?" For me, what comes to mind is a woman on my block. I thought we were friends and through a long series of circumstances, which I will not get into here, she's been really cold and distant. I don't know why. I don't know what I've done. OK, that experience could work here. I will choose that one.

Bridging Your Memories to Your Character

So now that you've chosen your memory, you've got to ground your character's reality in yours. You have to bridge the two memories so they become one. But how do you literally connect your memories to your characters?

This is how I do it. I'm playing Danny Zuko and I have got to be confused and the memory I've chosen is the one with my neighbor. Now that I've chosen my "bridgey" memory, I sit in a comfortable chair, close my eyes, and remember everything I can about any recent interaction I have had with her. I use all of my senses to remember. I taste, touch, smell, hear, and feel the memory. And just as soon as I've got that picture in my heart and mind, I think of the script and the scene where I'm confused. I then open my eyes. I might need to do this exercise a time or seven. Eventually I won't even need to think of my neighbor at all. My confusion over Sandy will become so real to me.

Let's try another memory, shall we? If we were playing Maria, she's afraid of her feelings for the captain. She's scared to love him. Seems weird to me that anyone would be scared to love someone. But I'm an actor and I have to empathize so I can play the part. I need to go through my memories and see if there was ever a time I was afraid to love someone. I remember a time when my husband and I were first dating and he said he loved me, but I was terrified to admit that I loved him too. Loving my husband wasn't in my life plan. Yep. That memory fits. I will use that one. Now back to my comfy chair. I sit. I close my eyes. I remember every sense until it's real. I scene associate, I open my eyes. Try it. Take any moment of a character's life, whether you're watching a movie or TV show or reading a book, and see if you can empathize and find a memory that's similar.

Step Three: Letting It All Go

"Acting is not about dressing up. Acting is about stripping bare. The whole essence of learning lines is to forget them so you can make them sound like you thought of them that instant."
— Glenda Jackson

What I'm about to say now might really perplex you. Are you ready? Let go of all the homework you've done during rehearsals and do your best to stay in the moment.

You see, I believe that the rehearsal process is about finding your character. And as you build the memories and create intentions and do your prep work, all of that is working its way through your subconscious. In a way, all the work stuff actors do is giving your brain something to do, like busy work, while your heart integrates the character. Letting go is the ultimate exercise in trust. You have to believe so much in what you've done, that you know your character will arise instinctively when you walk onstage in front of the audience.

Live in the Moment

Ah, a challenging actor's lesson and a good life lesson: don't think about what you're going to say next or do next. Experience right now. Because truly there is no past and there is no future, those are the illusion. All that really exists is now. That, to me, is the actor's goal.

Chapter Seven

Acting from the Outside In

The World According to Flip

The first Showdown director you heard from was me, so, like, "hi."
It's now time to hear from the second Showdown director, Flip. Flip is
my husband and writing partner, but in his younger, mime days he
studied with Richmond Shepherd, one of the foremost mime dudes,
which led Flip to tour the country, performing in cities all over the East,
as a mime. My point to this pontification of Flip's history is that his
"actor" approach is physical. It comes from his mime training.

Said another way, Flip works from the outside in. This means that he
finds a physical mannerism for the character and then builds the
character's emotions from that place. Here's an example. Flip played
Cooper, the singing cowboy in our musical *Wild Dust*. He began his
character preparation with Cooper's bowlegged cowboy walk. He then
asked himself, "Why is Cooper bowlegged?" The obvious answer:
because Cooper rides horses. Why does he ride horses? The answer was
that Cooper rides horses 'cause he's a lawman in the West. Well, why is
he a lawman? Well, he's a lawman, because ... Do you see? From a
physical bit, Cooper is a cowboy, so he walks bowlegged, so Flip began
to build the heart and soul of the character.

Now Flip's approach to a character is just as valid as my approach.
It's up to you to decide which, if either, you like better. Remember, use
what works for you, toss what doesn't. You're on a life journey of
learning and growth.

Relaxation Exercises

'Tis difficult to create anything if you're stressed or tense, so whether
your character work will be internal, external, or Martian, you must be
relaxed. There are many different kinds of relaxation exercises and you
can learn them from dance or meditation or yoga classes. Here be a few
exercises that I do with my actors.

Body Stretching

First, and muy importante, is that you don't bounce when you are
stretching. The point of these exercises is to stretch the muscle and
release the tension. So stretch enough to release and nothing more. Our
goal is to get you relaxed, not built like a bodybuilder. I also recommend

that you get to rehearsals fifteen minutes early and find a quiet place where you can do these exercises. They're wonderful for bringing you into the here and now and letting go of all the other junk that might be spinning about in your head. Oh, and it's OK to listen to peaceful music while you do these exercises.

1. Find a quiet place where you can stretch out.
2. The first part of these exercises is done standing. The second half you will sit. So for now, stand with your eyes closed.
3. Take a deep breath. In through your nose, nice and slow. Now breathe out through your nose, nice and slow. Do this three or four times. Breathe in for three to five seconds and breathe out for three to five seconds. It's OK to count to yourself as you breathe in and out. The purpose of breathing is to connect you to your body and let go of your mind.
4. It's now time to relax your neck. First, gently drop your head forward. Feel the weight of your head pulling towards the earth. Now, roll your head so that it rests on your left shoulder. Is there tension in the right side of your neck when you do this? Imagine every exhalation of your breath loosens your tight neck muscles and releases the tension. Breathe like this for three or four breaths. In through the nose, out through the nose. Now roll your head slowly to the other shoulder. Let your head rest on the right shoulder. Is there tension in the left side of your neck? Again, use your breath to loosen the tight muscles. Finally, roll your head back and forth from shoulder to shoulder. Notice any tension? Breathe into it and then release it with the out breath. Continue to gently roll your head three or four times. Reverse the motion of your head roll, this time going right to left. Do that three or four times. Remember to breathe. In through your nose and out through your nose.
5. Relax your shoulders. While continuing your easy in and out breathing, roll your shoulders forward, gently, three to five times, then roll them back gently, three to five times.
6. Release the tension in your back. Reach up to the sky, feet on tiptoes, reaching and stretching your fingers up and up and up. Look up as you do this and let your jaw drop. Reach. Reach. Reach. Now release. Hands at your sides. Breathe in and breathe out.
7. Stretch out your sides. Put your right hand on your hip then reach your left hand over your head so your arm is shaped like a C with your palm down towards the earth. Now lean to the right. Feel the stretch in your left side. Again, don't strain, just reach and

breathe. Give it a count of twenty. Release. Now do the other side. Put your left hand on your left hip, right hand goes over your head with palm facing down, lean. Feel the stretch in your right side. Give it a count of twenty, release.

The next section of exercises will be done sitting on the floor.

8. Stretch the groin and hips. Put the soles of your feet together so you're legs are in a diamond-ish shape. This stretch is done with a flat back. Don't bounce! With souls of the feet together, bend from the hips, back is slightly arched, and the head is slightly lifted. You will feel the stretch in your groin. Breathe in and out. Remember, this is not a competition. This is a relaxation exercise and the point is to relax and loosen up any muscles that are tight. If you feel tightness in the groin, breathe into it. Imagine your out breaths are loosening the muscles and allowing you to bend further. Ahhhh. Do this for a count of twenty.

9. Loosen up the shoulders and outer back. Open your legs so they look like a V. With legs extended, still sitting on the floor, reach your left hand to your right ankle. Grab your ankle and gently pull. Feel the stretch in the muscles in your back and shoulders. Now if you can't reach your right ankle, that's OK. Grab your right calf or thigh with your left hand. Hold the stretch for twenty seconds, remembering to breathe. Switch sides. Right hand grabbing left ankle. Hold for twenty seconds.

10. Loosen your fingers. Bend and stretch your fingers for a count of twenty. Open and close your hands. Now stretch your hands as far apart as your fingers will allow. Release. Do this one more time. Scrunch your fingers into a tight fist. Scrunch. Scrunch and release. Again. Do this one more time.

11. Stand. Do you feel any pricks of tension in your body? Breathe into them and out of them. Rotate them. First one way and then the other. Remember, be very gentle with yourself.

12. Stretch the face muscles. Open your mouth as wide as it will go then close it. Rotate your jaw open and close three to four times. Scrunch up your face until it's really pruney and tight. Hold it for five to ten seconds. Release.

Body relaxed. Mind calmer. It's time to build a character from the outside in.

Gotta Have a Gimmick

Every person has a *hook,* a mannerism that is unique to them. Michael Keaton, who played Batman, chews toothpicks. David Schwimmer, Ross from *Friends,* has that nasal whine to his voice. Dustin

Hoffman, *The Graduate,* has a slight bounce to his walk. Characters are the same as people. Lucy in *You're a Good Man, Charlie Brown* bends and shouts at her prey. Harry Potter pushes up his glasses. Tarzan beats his chest.

What Is Your Character's Hook?

With some characters it's easy to find their hook: you're playing a cowboy, you know you'll walk bowlegged; you're an Edwardian women, you'll curtsey whenever you greet someone; a gangstah will grab his crotch.

The simplest method for finding a character's signature move is to go to the script. Usually the playwright will give you clues. In the musical *You're a Good Man, Charlie Brown,* Linus always has his blanket. In the play *Ordinary People,* our young hero tried to commit suicide by cutting his wrist. In our comedy *Ghost of a Chance,* the heroine, Bethany, chews gum whenever she's nervous, which is often — she's a real chain chewer.

Once you've figured out what the hook is, ask yourself those two mondo important questions: how does my character feel about that and why does my character do this? By following that chain of questions, you will uncover the emotional core of your character.

Let's go back to Linus. He carries a blanket. Why does he carry a blanket? He loves his blanket. Why does he love his blanket? The blanket makes him feel safe. How does he feel about needing to be safe? Embarrassed, but he can't help it. He knows he shouldn't need a blanket, but the blankey gives him such comfort. Why does he need comfort? His big sister Lucy is a bully. How does he feel about his sister Lucy? He's afraid she'll hit him, but he loves her. Why does he love her? Do you see? You follow the train of why until a picture is created for you.

 Aha Moment!

There is no right or wrong answer to your why questions. They are simply choices you make. And the more you can relate to the choices, the more real your character will become.

What if you decided that Linus loves his blanket because it's pretty and he has issues about his appearance or he loves his blanket because it smells good and reminds him of his grandmother? Any could be valid choices. The best choice is the one that you can connect with *and* serves the show.

The Animal Within

Let's say the script offers you no clue at all. Your character is written as an amorphous blob. No fear, there are other ways to build the physicality of your character.

Everyone reminds us of someone else ... or something else. We compare humans to animals all the time: he's as slow as a sloth or as clumsy as a puppy or as graceful as a cheetah. My son has a teacher who makes me think of a hummingbird. His teacher is thin and pretty and her mannerisms are quick; she flits, she doesn't walk. Many people have said I remind them of a large momma cat like a lion or a tigress, because I'm ferocious when it comes to my cubs. Characters based on animals can be imaginative, unusual, and very, very real.

So first things first, what animal does your character remind you of? Danny Zuko reminds me of a lion, not the leader of the pack, but a young upstart lion that's looking to own the tribe. Maria reminds me of a butterfly. And Lucy from *Charlie Brown* reminds me of a shark.

Once you've decided which animal your character reminds you of, it's time to study that type of animal. The more specific the animal you observe, the more real will be your character. Let me show you what I mean. Let's say I was playing Superman. The first question I'd ask myself is what animal does the man in blue remind me of? My answer: he reminds me of a collie. Cool. Superman is like a collie. Wait, which collie? Is the collie a pure breed or a mix? And if he's a mutt, what other breeds are there? Is he an old collie or a puppy? Is my collie the alpha or the runt? And a collie doing what? Is the collie saving the house or cowering because he ate out of the trash?

Animals are as distinct as humans. My golden retriever, Waiter (the beast), is not like Ginger, the golden down the street. My Waiter is willful, affectionate, clueless, and runs in circles like a cyclone when he's excited about anything. He also talks when we come home. He whimpers and whines and tells us about his day. Do you see? When choosing an animal, be specific. No generic bear or penguin. If you must, go to the zoo and find the animal.

As long as your animal is specific, it doesn't have to be a living, breathing animal. It can be an animated animal. For my Superman I have chosen the collie from *101 Dalmatians.* I think his name is King and he tells the Dalmatians about the puppies. But I didn't just arbitrarily choose an animated animal. I have reasons:

- Superman isn't real, so I wanted to base him on a slightly unworldly animal.
- Dogs are likable, loyal, and loved by many, like Superman.
- This particular dog is brave and deeply cares about the state of the world, like Superman.

Remember, it's important to know why you are making the choices you are making.

So now that I know which animal I've chosen and why I've chosen him, it's time to find the moment in my animal's life when he most resembles the character I'm playing. Said another way, is my character most like my animal when he's sleeping, eating, hunting, mating, playing ... you get the idea.

Back to my Man of Steel. I chose my animated collie 'cause to me he would be doing exactly what Superman does: protect the pack. He sits up straight, sniffs a lot, and makes no unnecessary movements 'cause he has to be ready to pounce at any time.

Awesome. I've chosen my animal and what action he's engaged in. It's time for me to become my animal. I think this is the most challenging part for many an actor. Uncomfortable with their bodies or the idea that they could be an animal, they play at the animal, pretending but not fully embracing. Does this make sense? They act at it. Actors will put fingers up on their heads as ears or hold their hand by their butt so they have a tail, but really, animals don't do that. They're born with those physical traits. The question to ask yourself, again, is why. Why does my animal have a tail? Why does he have ears that stand up instead of droop? Why does he lick his fur or nuzzle or lift his leg? Why? Your job as an actor is to *be* the animal, not *act like* the animal.

Fun. I mean, woof!

Now that you've practiced being your animal, the last thing you must do is humanize it. In other words, find the traits your animal has that you think your character would use and use them. But whatever mannerism you choose has to have an emotional connection to your character.

So for my Superman I chose sniffing, because the superhero is not from earth and this world is very different than the one he comes from, plus I think dangerous people emit different scents than harmless people and I think that could help my Superman. Translation: whenever I'm onstage as Superman and I think there might be danger, I'm going to sniff. I might also run around in circles three times before I eat or jump around when I'm excited, but for now, I'm only going to sniff.

Aha Moment!

Everything you do is a choice.
Every decision you make or don't make is a choice.
Simply because you are not consciously saying, "I choose this" doesn't mean you're not choosing. Failure to decide on something is making a choice too — not deciding. So make a choice.

The Emotions Within

Choosing an animal isn't the only way to physicalize a character. Everyone emanates one very strong emotion. You ever been to a party and met someone who gave you a weird vibe or a good vibe? That's what I'm talking about. It's an overriding energy. If you met me, you'd probably say I was intense. My passions and dislikes are strong and when you meet me you know I'm going to have a feeling about something. It's different for different people. Some people are always sad. Others confused. A few lucky souls are happy.

First question is what is your overriding emotion? What feeling do you have more times than not? Remember, this "emotion" isn't bad. And it isn't good. It just is.

Your Character's Emotion

Like you, your character will have an emotion as well. I would say Superman's emotion would be anger. Righteous anger. For our lovely Maria Von Trapp, it's probably devotion. It isn't always easy to know what a character's overriding emotion is. Sometimes it takes a little playing around with feelings before you find it.

Finding the Emotion Game

Purpose of the game:
See what your emotions "look" like.

Directions:
This game is played in three steps.
Step One:
1. On a plethora of little pieces of paper, write down every emotion you can think of. Start simple. Anger. Rage. Sadness. Joy. One emotion for each piece of paper.

2. Place the pieces of paper in an empty box or hat.
3. While standing in front of a mirror, pick out one of the pieces of paper.
4. Strike and hold a position that expresses that emotion.

At first you might feel a bit goofy doing this in front of a mirror — keep at it. Eventually you'll forget it's you you're looking at. Oh, and remember to make the emotion real. Search and find the true feeling inside yourself.

Step Two:

1. Get more little pieces of paper, write down every emotion you can think of, but make these emotions more complex. Grief. Paranoia. Shame. One emotion per piece of paper.
2. Place the papers in an empty box.
3. Draw a piece of paper.
4. In front of a mirror, recreate the emotion.

Step Three:

1. Little papers, write down abstract emotions. Victory. Energy. Courage.
2. Draw. Strike. Pose.

Character Emotion Game

Purpose of the game:
Find your character's emotion.

Directions:

1. Read the script. Two times at least.
2. Close your eyes and imagine your character is sitting across from you having a latte.
3. What is he talking about?
4. What expression do you see on his face? In his eyes? Are his eyes crinkled with confusion? Is his forehead riddled with worry? Is he beaming at you, glowing with joy? What does his body look like? What's his posture? What position are his shoulders? Are they hunched or high?
5. In a word, determine what feeling he's conveying. Is it mad? Sad? Glad? Afraid?
6. Open your eyes.
7. In front of a mirror, convey his emotion. In other words, express the feeling you got from him.
8. Ask yourself, "Is there anything more I can do with my body to convey his emotion?" If you sensed sadness, could your shoulders be more hunched? If you picked up on mad, your fists

might be clenched. Happy? You're standing straight and smiling from ear to ear.

9. Ask yourself, "Why does my character feel this way and why does he express the feeling like this?" Oh let's say you felt he was afraid. And his brow was wrinkled like a Sharpei. Why does he crease his forehead? Is he nearsighted and doesn't know it and so when he's afraid his sight is the first thing to go? Which might mean that every time he gets worried about something he might become slightly blind. You now have a place to begin for your character. Keep going. Create a fretful walk and a fearful voice. But always ask yourself, "Why?" Why does he do this? Why?

Wow! A lot of physical work. You need nourishment. I'm seeing a slice of thick crusted pizza, cheese only, or a big old slice of seedless watermelon.

One Gesture

Creating movement isn't the only way to use your body. There's not using movement too. I love this approach because it's physical, but it really makes you notice every gesture.

Clean Moves Game

Purpose of the game:

Get rid of all that unnecessary junky movement.

Directions:

You will need a monologue — any monologue will do — and someone to watch you.

1. Standing in front of your watching person, do the monologue without moving a muscle. Not a twitch. Oh OK, you can blink your eyes, but nothing more. That's it.

2. Now do the mono again. And you may use one gesture. It might be you raise your arm or nod your head or turn to the right. But you only get one. *Uno! One. Single.* Pick that gesture wisely, 'cause for the whole mono you get only one.

3. Read the monologue again, but you may have three gestures this time: turn your head, stomp your foot, and jump, or you might nod, spin, and wave an arm. But you only get three. That's it.
4. Finally, do the monologue again and you're free to move about.

Uh-huh, how did that feel? Did you find that you really didn't need all the movement you thought you did? I know. Weird, huh?

Aha Moment!

Less is more
How many times have we heard this? But nowhere could it be more appropriate than acting. Think about the dude who does the classic slipping on the banana peel bit. The first actor comes in and his movements are clean and simple. He then slips, his feet go overhead, and he falls in one clean sweep. The second actors' movements are frenetic. He slips then slides then wiggles his feet and then tumbles. Which actor is funnier? The one who moved less than the other. Always. You got to keep it to a minimum. Remember, one move is always better than four.

Tips for the Rehearsal Process

As a physical actor, your approach to the role might be slightly different than the cerebral actor, but it is equally valid. Here are a few tips.

Walk the Walk

Because how you stand, how you walk, affects how people perceive you — and how you perceive yourself — shoes are an important factor in your characterization. Talk to the costumer, to the director, your mother (just joking — although call her, it would mean a lot to hear from you). Find out what your character would put on his feet and start working in them. It will help tremendously.

Blocking

When it comes to blocking, start in big bold strokes — traffic patterns — and then slowly add the detail. *Traffic patterns* are a shorthand way of saying you know where your exits, entrances, and marks are, but that's about it. Once you have a pretty strong grasp of your traffic patterns, it's time to take your movement to the next level and add silhouettes. *Silhouettes* are pictures viewed by the audience. So, if you're standing next to an actor, what kind of an image are you conveying to the audience?

For example, you are playing a singing cowboy and you've been asked to stand beside your fair lady and sing to her. How do you stand to create the most relevant singing cowboy picture? You might hitch your foot up on a nearby chair so you can hold your guitar better, you might lean a little into her to show her that you've taken a likin' to her, you might wink at her now and then. You would not stand straight, hold the guitar down by your waist, and stare at her blankly. Does this make sense? And do this every time you're asked to stand on a stage and have a scene. Every time you're asked to cross. You're aware of what your body is saying to the audience.

Delve into the World of the Character

There is no place like a character's home. And the more you learn about that home/world, the more you can draw from. So immerse yourself in character land. If you are an Austrian girl from a convent, listen to Austrian music, eat Austrian food, speak to Austrian people, and sleep in a bare essential room. If you're an alien from another planet, go to some place otherworldly. Vazquez Rocks is great if you live in Southern California. Or go someplace where little English is spoken and see if you can understand or communicate with the locals.

Energy

Energy. Energy. Energy. A lethargic performance is a boring performance. So do whatever you must to keep that energy flowing. To get your energy up, you can run in place, you can run around backstage, you can breathe deeply as if you were going underwater for a deep dive, or you can eat carbs. However, do not outpace your fellow actors. Be aware of the energy they are giving and do your best to only one up them, not a trillion up them, or you will look hyper by comparison.

Projection and Diction

It truly doesn't matter which approach you take to your character, if the audience can't hear you or understand what you're saying, it's pointless. So speak loudly and clearly.

Why?

Acting, like life, is a series of choices. Make sure everything you do has a solid reason behind it. And if you don't know, that's OK. Find out. Or make another choice that you can justify.

 **GOLD STAR**

For creating an amazing, memorable character that is completely your own. Yay for you! Go to the back of the book, color a stone. Any color you like. It's your star.

Chapter Eight

Acting through Song

From Dennis' POV

Dennis is Showdown's musical director. He is a brilliant musician with tons of credits including *The Suite Life of Zack and Cody* and *Earth Girls Are Easy* plus lots of published musicals. But what makes Dennis an exceptional musical director is that he was an actor early in his career, so he approaches singing as an actor. Translation: he knows how terrifying singing is to most young actors and he has found an approach that makes actors feel safe when they sing. Truly …

Alba was a cheerleader with a wide smile and a barrel full of confidence, except when it came to singing. Poor girl. She was horrified at the thought of singing a tune. And when faced with the assignment of singing in Dennis' class, her fear literally drove her to tears. Alba would get up to sing, get three words out, and start to cry. Tears fell like rain. "I can't do this. Please don't make me," she'd plead. She simply could not sing. Dennis, being Dennis, understood. He told her to sing just three words, which she did, but there were more tears. Every day from then till the end of camp, Dennis made her get up and sing three more words. Every time she sang, he'd support her, applaud her, and reassure her that she could do this. At the end of three weeks, Alba overcame her terror and began auditioning for musicals. Yep. Musicals. Lo and behold, she got cast and she is now a singing fool.

Anybody Can Sing

Dennis' approach to confident singing begins with understanding why you feel the way you do. Sound familiar? By knowing why you feel the way you feel, you can rebuild your confidence. So let's go into your memory drawer and find the doubt about singing … For most people, it's because some insecure nimrod told them, "Please don't sing," "Shut up," or "Ew, you can't sing." And the trauma stuck. They stopped singing. The fear grew.

But who was that nimrod that shaped your vocal career? And why did he say, "Stop singing"? Was he an expert? Not likely. Probably he was a "protective friend" who secretly wished he could sing, but was afraid, so silenced you instead of face his own fear. Or the nimrod was a teacher who didn't know how to help improve your voice so instead of admitting she was unable, she silenced you, the singer.

So really, those shushing people, when they said you can't, they were really saying *they* can't. Does that make sense? Let me explain it this way: when someone tells you to be quiet, it's because *they* can't handle the noise, not because the noise is unpleasant. Think about it. How many times have giggling children been asked to hush? Giggles are a delicious noise to some of us, but to the silencer they are like nails on a chalkboard and must be quieted.

It's not about you; it's about them. And if you understand that, you know that they asked you to stop singing not 'cause your voice wasn't pretty, but because they couldn't handle it for whatever reason. This means that *you can sing!* And if you dream of being an amazing musical theatre performer, you can be. It's totally up to you. Dennis says so.

Singing Requires Support

There are some coaches who will say to sing you must, "Sing from your diaphragm!" Other directors will say, "Open your vocal chords!" Others who will say, well, other things. The point to what everybody is saying is *support.* Singing requires muscles that can support your voice.

What are those muscles? I went to Google and here's what I found out … The diaphragm is the main breath support muscle and it sits under your rib cage. Take a deep breath in and then breathe out. Notice how your breath is released in a steady stream of air, but there's a slight resistance. This is due to the constant tension in the diaphragm. The tension in the diaphragm is there to slow down the release of air from your lungs. This is mondo important to musicians who play wind instruments like the flute or clarinet and singers 'cause if the breath were released too rapidly, then the musician or the singer could not hold a note. Whoa, so what that means is that the diaphragm controls the breath.

To create more breath or deeper breathing, the diaphragm pushes on the stomach as you breathe out and literally pulls at the bottom of the lungs. So this means that the diaphragm needs to be worked like any other muscle so it can push harder on the stomach and pull more of the lungs so you can have more air to sing. Wow.

Now take uno momento por favor (a moment please) and place your hands under your rib cage. Sometimes it's easier to do this when you're lying down. Imagine your diaphragm as you're doing this. Now say, "Ahhhh." If you feel the muscle underneath vibrating, then you have met your diaphragm. Say, "Hi, diaphragm."

Trivia
Michael Crawford, the legendary singer who created the Phantom in *Phantom of the Opera*, was performing the Phantom. He was doing the song with Christine where they're on the boat and there are candles in the water. Anywho, there's Mr. M singing, pretending to push the boat, when the boat decides to stop working. Now Michael is in the middle of the stage, in front of a live audience, singing this haunting melody to get his lady across stage and the boat ain't havin' any. He uses the stick in his hands to shove the boat, but the vessel whines in return. He pushes harder, still singing, and the boat goes wacky. It actually starts spinning in circles. Then it turns backwards. Michael isn't sure what to do, so he keeps singing. And singing. And singing. In the end, the song took three times as long as it should have, but hey, he was able to carry on the entire time, 'cause he had the breath support.

To Take Vocal Lessons or Not to Take Vocal Lessons

Both Hamlet and Dennis say a resounding "yes!" Take vocal lessons. The teacher will give you techniques to build that support muscle. And they should also build your confidence. But before you go seeking out a coach, a few tips.

1. Interview the teacher. Ask them lots and lots of questions: how long have they been teaching, what is their philosophy about teaching, how much homework will there be … Finding a good singing teacher is like finding a good doctor. You want someone who makes you feel comfortable, yet you know is knowledgeable.

2. Ask for and call the referrals. A good teacher will have other students who are willing to sing the teacher's praises. You want to know why they like their teacher, and what, if anything, they don't like about their teacher.

3. See if you can audit a lesson or watch a lesson free of charge. Some teachers may say no, and some may offer you a free introduction. You won't know unless you ask.

4. You will want to find out about cost. High price doesn't necessarily equate with the best teacher.

5. Again, there is no right or wrong teacher; there is only the teacher that feels right to you. Trust your guts. You will know.

You can find a vocal coach at many a place:

- *Choir.* Yep. Your school choir department is a great place to improve your singing technique and it's free, so join the choir.
- *Colleges.* Vocal students eager to pay for their tuition will be happy to teach you what they know for a fee. To find a qualified college student, call the college choir department and ask.
- *Online.* Type in "vocal instructors" for your area and look at all the names that pop up. This method of finding a teacher is a bit trickier 'cause you don't know these coaches from your cousin Adam. If you choose to go this route, make sure to ask for those precious referrals — and call them! You want to make sure this teacher is for real.
- *Referrals.* This is my favorite method of finding a vocal coach. Fellow actors, directors, and teachers will always know someone they think rocks. Ask and ye shall find.

Speaking of referrals … a teacher that I love is Carolyn Fallin. She can be found at www.vocalImage.com. She's great with young people and she's incredibly talented.

So now that you know you can sing, you understand a bit more about how you sing, and you've found a great vocal coach to help you sing. It's time to take your voice on the road by …

Auditioning for a Musical

It is amazing how many actors get eliminated from casting for the silliest reasons. They don't think they can sing so they don't try out, which is not you anymore 'cause you know you can sing. They don't audition well, which isn't going to be you 'cause you have this book to tell you …

How to Give an Awesome Audition

Proper preparedness for a singing audition comes in two phases: the pre-audition and the actual audition. Let's start with what you need to do. Before you audition you need to: cast your song properly; be precise in your song; show range, dynamics, and emotion; and practice your audition song.

Cast Your Song Properly

When auditioning for a musical you will sing a song of your choice. This means that you want to sing a song that is appropriate for your age. You are a lovely young person, so find a song that a teen would sing. Choose a song that you might sing in a show. In other words, yes, you may feel you really know Tevye's pain in the song, "If I Were a Rich Man," but you will not likely be cast as an aging, Jewish milkman until you're well into your forties. If you must sing a song from *Fiddler,* how about Motel the tailor's song "Miracle of Miracles" or the classic song "Matchmaker?"

In addition to *Fiddler,* there are many roles out there for young people. Here are a few wonderful shows with songs perfect for your age: *High School Musical* (a bit overdone, but it's your age), *Urinetown, The Sound of Music, The Secret Garden, Thirteen.* And then there are the Showdown shows: *Quixote, Nottingham, Mirror Image.* Go to Contemporary Drama Service, Meriwether Publishing, Pioneer Drama, or Dramatic and you will find a lot more shows.

Be Precise with Your Song

When auditioning you will be asked to sing sixteen bars of your song. Not eighteen, not twenty-four, but sixteen. You must choose the sixteen bars that highlight your voice. Don't worry if you don't sing the chorus. Make sure you choose the best sixteen bars for you.

Show Range, Dynamics, and Emotion

What are these things? Let me explain, grasshoppa.
• *Range* is how low and high your voice can go.
• *Dynamics* means the peaks and valleys of a song — soft and loud.
• *Emotions* are finding the story of the song and connecting with it.
Of the three, emotion is probably the most important element of choosing a song. You want to pick a tune that you emotionally connect with. Most of the great vocal performances that I have seen didn't come from a flawless singer.

Trivia

Jean Simmons, not the singer from KISS, who starred in the movie *Guys and Dolls* with Frank Sinatra, performed in Steven Sondheim's *A Little Night Music.* Her song was "Send In The Clowns." I still remember sitting in the audience and seeing Jean walk out in that red sequined gown. She took my breath away. Then she sang, and my gosh, I was only a teenager, but I knew what she was talking about. I understood. Her rendition was eternal and I shall never forget it. But could she "sing"? There are many who say her voice lacked perfect technique. Hmmmm. Her performance was so amazing that to this day I remember it.

Practice Your Audition Song

And practice. And practice again. If you're told you are going to audition for a musical in six days, practice every day. An hour a day. Be as familiar with the hills and valleys of that song as you can. Know it. Live it. Breathe it. *Practice!*

Be prepared with a karaoke CD of your song, but if possible you should also have the sheet music. At many auditions, a rehearsal accompanist will be provided. It is up to you to mark out the sixteen bars on the sheet music that the accompanist will need to play. And you have to have the song converted to the right key. For girls, the best key is somewhere between B and D. For boys, E, F, G, and A are usually good keys. You are prepared, oh wise one, it's now time to go and audition.

At the Audition

1. *Find a quiet place* and do a few relaxation exercises to get centered and present.
2. *Warm up your voice.* It's always a good idea to warm up your voice, whether you're auditioning or prepping for a rehearsal. One great exercise is to blow your lips, like a raspberry, and then hum the scales through the raspberryness of your lips
3. *Limit your movement.* Don't do a lot of fancy dancin'. A step or two to underscore an emotion is OK, but that's it. The directors want to know if you can sing, not if you can dance.
4. *Be concise.* Avoid aimless chitchat. Come in and say your name. You can say the name of the song or not, sometimes they'll ask you. If they do, tell them. When you're done, say "thank you." And walk out. You want to look as professional as possible.

Musical Rehearsals

You've been cast. Of course. You came in and knocked the director's socks off with your rendition of "You Made Me Love You." Wow! Yay for you. So what can you expect during the rehearsal process? Musical rehearsals are not that different than straight play rehearsals, except you need to add in time to learn and rehearse singing and dancing.

The First Day of Rehearsal

The first day will be the table read. You will read through the play (also called The Book), and you will hear the songs from the show. A wise actor will follow the etiquette he learned earlier in this book: don't text or talk during the reading, ask questions, listen to answers, bring pen and paper *and* a small tape recorder which will come in handy when learning the songs. The only thing the wise actor will need to do at a musical table read that he didn't do at a straight play read is applaud the songs. This is especially important if it's an original show. The writers will be there and they really love the accolades.

After the table read, actors are given either the score (that's the sheet music for the show), the vocal script (just the vocals and melody lines), or a karaoke CD of the show.

The Second Day of Rehearsal

Again, it varies from director to director. Some shows the director dives right in right after the table read and begins working the show. Other times, the "rehearsals" begin on the second day. Doesn't matter how the calendar breaks down. The next phase of a musical rehearsal is usually learning the songs, typically taught to you by the music director.

Make sure to warm up your voice. The music director should help you with this, but if he fails to, make sure you remember. You can do scales or the raspberry warm up or any other exercise your vocal teacher has taught you.

Once you've been taught your songs, it's up to you to learn the music and lyrics outside of rehearsals. So if you thought, "Wow, the CD of the show would make a great Frisbee for Fido" or "The score would be an awesome liner for the birdcage," then think again. These are learning tools. Use them. Oh, and also use your little hand recorder. It will help tremendously when you are reviewing any harmonies or such that you were taught.

Approaching Your Character in a Musical

Why Sing?

As an actor, you need to figure out why your character must sing when talking would suffice. Ask yourself, what is so important to my character that speaking isn't enough? Why would my character's thoughts or feelings require music? Make sense? In *The Sound of Music*, Maria must sing "The Sound of Music" because she's so overcome with joy at the beauty of the mountains, simply saying, "I love the mountains" won't do. In *Grease*, "Freddie My Love" is a sad lament that the character can't share with her friends, yet still affects her deeply.

The Emotions of the Songs

Just like characters have an overriding emotion, so does every musical score. For example, *Sweeney Todd's* emotional baseline is dark and brooding. *Annie Get Your Gun* is upbeat and hopeful. Your musical performance needs to be in line with the emotional baseline of the musical score. Said another way, you wouldn't perform a comedic number in *Les Misérables* the same way you'd perform a comedic number from *A Funny Thing Happened on the Way to the Forum*. In *Les Mis*, your comedy would be darker and smaller, whereas in *Forum* your performance would be broad and big and silly. You need to tweak your performance towards the tone of the show. Make sense?

The Emotions of the Character

Every part matters, chorus to "star," (I say "star" with a catch in my throat, 'cause there is no great "starring" performance without a great ensemble.) Said another way, your part matters. Even if all you're given is Second Spear Carrier From the Left. That spear carrier matters. Why is he second? Why not first? Does he want to be first? Why? Why is he a spear carrier and not a knife thrower? Approach your character the way you would any other acting role.

Remember these questions:

Who is your character?

What is your character's intention?

Where is your character coming from?

How does your character feel about the other characters?

And of course, know what you feel and why. Truly, the size of the character matters little to the audience. I have worked with actors who made one line so memorable the actor got a standing ovation.

Trivia

David Hyde Pierce, many of you know him as Frasier's brother on the show *Frasier*, wasn't suppose to be Niles. In fact, there wasn't going to be a younger brother, but David did such an awesome job at his audition, they had to write a role for him. And then there's Gary Burghoff of *M.A.S.H.* fame. His role of Radar O'Reilly was supposed to be a walk-on. He did so much with it, they expanded the part. And last but not least, remember the movie *Up?* Kevin the bird had nary a line, but without him, the story could not have unfolded. He was that important to the plot!

So the question I ask of you, my lovely, is what can you do with the role you've been given?

Aha Moment!

Your performance is a gift to the audience.

No matter which role you play, whenever you get up in front of an audience, you have a chance to give the audience an amazing gift. You can take them to magical places. You are their guide to Disneyland and Magic Mountain and the Leaning Tower of Pisa all rolled into one. Wow!

Voice-Over Work

There is more than one way to give a great vocal performance: you can sing in a choir, you can sing in a band, or you can do voice-over work. Voice-over work is exactly as it sounds, acting over a microphone. The audience can't see you, but they can hear your voice. Performing in radio plays, doing animated characters, playing announcers, and radio personalities are all considered voice-over work. What's awesome about this kind of acting is you don't have to worry about wearing makeup or having lines memorized because the "performance" is done in a studio. Stars love to do voice-over work. It pays great and they don't have to look pretty. And most actors think the work is pretty straightforward. Maybe it is for them, but not the rest of the crew.

Trivia

When we were doing the sequel to *Hunchback*, Demi Moore didn't want to fly into Disney, so the director flew to her hometown and recorded her performance as Esmeralda in her home studio. All should have gone as planned, except Demi had very different ideas from the director as to how she wanted to play her character. The director needed her to shout "I love you!" to Kevin Kline's Phoebus at the end of the movie. But she didn't feel her character would do that. Hmmmm. Kevin Kline had already been recorded shouting, "I love you," so it would look unromantic if she didn't shout back. The director had a real dilemma on his hands. Did he push and risk alienating Demi or did he rerecord Kevin? The director decided to reconceive the ending. Kevin still shouted, but Demi would whisper, "I love you!" in her beloved's ear. Demi liked that. So the director redrew the scene for Demi. He did the storyboards right there in her living room. Demi was happy. The director was happy. All was said and done ... *not!* The director then said, "Wouldn't it be funny if Demi now shouted 'I love you' while she was close to Phoebus' ear?" Demi said "Yes!" That would be funny. She then did a take of shouting, "I love you!" believing that her character was in close to Kevin's character. Ah, but what many don't know is that the director, now having his take of the shouting Esmeralda, threw away the storyboards done in Demi's living room and went back to his original vision.

Getting Started
To get started with voice-over work, you will need five to six character voices. Make sure the voices are distinct, meaning you don't want one voice to be from the deep south and the other from the upper south. Make the characters as different as you possibly can, like one might be a three-year-old Martian and the other an old lady from the Bronx. Variety is the key to getting voice-over work.

The Character Voice Game
Purpose of the game:
Create as many character voices as you can.

Directions:
1. Say the line, "The rain in Spain stays mainly in the plain."
2. Now say the same line as a four year old.
3. Say the same line as a mouse, a 100-year-old man, and an alien.
4. If you're male, say the line as a female and if you're female, say the line as a boy might.
5. Now add an emotion to the character. A mad mouse, a lonely 100-year-old man, a happy alien. Just don't forget to ask yourself why your character feels that way.

Trivia
Did you know that Audrey Hepburn did not do her own singing for *My Fair Lady*? That honor went to Marni Nixon, who went on to play Sister Sophia in *The Sound of Music*.

Dialects
Dialects are accents. I always find it funny that someone from England would think I have an accent. I don't, they do. But no, if I were in England, I would have an American accent, wouldn't I? It's easy to learn a new dialect if you listen.

The Dialect Game
Purpose of the game:
See if you can master a dialect.

Directions:
1. Go to the mall, the train station, or even your local Starbucks — anyplace where a variety of people might gather.

2. Find someone with an accent you don't recognize and listen. You can pretend to read a paper so it doesn't look like you're actually eavesdropping.

3. As they speak, quietly — shhhh, whisper — repeat what they say.

4. For the rest of the day, pepper your speech with their accent.

Another way to learn dialects is language CDs at the library. You can learn a new language and study a dialect at the same time. How cool is that?

Voice-Over Classes

Yep, classes in voice-over work do exist. You might need to do a bit of research to find one, but they're out there. I suggest you check out the Internet, type in "voice-over classes" for your area, and see what comes up. In addition, college extension programs sometimes offer them as well as community catalogues like parks and recreation.

Getting Voice-Over Work

Voice-over auditions are not like ordinary auditions. You don't come in and read for a director. Instead, you submit a demo. A demo is a sample of the different voices you can do. To create a decent demo, you'll need a studio. Most vocal instructors have one of those. In addition, a vocal instructor will be able to guide you through the process of creating a demo that sounds professional and where to submit the demo.

Silver Latte

Rest your vocal chords by drinking something warm and soothing. How about a cup of chamomile tea with a bit of lemon and honey? Or if the time is right, try one of Starbucks' seasonal blends, like a pumpkin or peppermint something.

Chapter Nine

Acting through Dance

*"Sure he was great, but don't forget Ginger Rogers did everything
he did backwards ... and in high heels!"*
— Bob Thaves, about legendary dancer Fred Astaire

The Way Domenic Sees It

If you cross Dick Van Dyke with a skinny Gene Kelley and throw in a ridiculous sense of humor, then you'd have Domenic, the Showdown choreographer. Domenic has been dancing since he was knee-high to a grasshopper. He's danced on cruise ships, stages, and in festivals. And what makes Domenic special as a choreographer is that he approaches dance as ... you guessed it ... an actor.

As actors have to find the emotion in the dialogue, dancers must find the emotion through the music and lyrics. For example, if the music is a tough rock throb, a dancer's moves would be more mechanical, rough. If the music comes in a soft 60s love song, a dancer would need to be more fluid. In other words, dancers are simply actors who express their character by dancing.

Aha Moment!

Every time you audition it's a chance to perform.
Never think of auditioning as being analyzed or having something to prove. Auditioning is a chance for you to share with whoever it is what you love to do. Always give it your all.

Dance Classes

Oh my gosh, you can find dance classes in: jazz, modern, ballet, tap, salsa, ballroom, hip-hop, bebop, and whatever other form tickles your fancy. The way cool thing about taking dance — any type of dance — is that it will help you as an actor, because dance increases body awareness. Actors who have studied dance are more graceful, they know what to do with their hands, they know how to walk without shuffling their feet, and their moves are clean. Plus dance is just a really fun way to exercise. And it's not expensive. You can find dance classes at the Y, the gym, your school, parks and recreation, extension courses, and if worse comes to worse, on your Wii. I cannot recommend dance classes enough. Start today!

What to Expect at a Dancer's Audition

You will enter a dark and cloudy room, there will be a single spotlight aimed directly into your eyes ... Ha! Just kidding. Dance auditions aren't that different from actor and singer auditions. Once you've warmed up, handed over your picture and résumé, you will be called into a stage or a big room with a group of other dancers. The dance captain will give you the combination. A *combination* is a series of dance steps that lasts somewhere between ten and twenty counts of eight; it's the choreography set to music.

You'll be taught the combination in counts of eight. You will not be given the whole routine all at once. The dance captain will continue to ask if you have any questions about what you're learning. It's OK to ask her to repeat a step so you feel you have it. Once you are taught the whole combination, she'll ask one final time for questions. If there are no questions, the entire group will then be split into two groups by the dance captain. This allows you to spread out and for the choreographer or whoever the powers that be to see you dance. You will be asked to do the combination a couple of times to music.

Your group will be split up again, this time into groups of three or four. You will do the routine again. Oy! Lots of times, huh? You will be asked to switch lines. Front to back and back to front. You will either be cut, which means they want to see you do a whole new routine, or told "thank you." But just 'cause you haven't made the cut doesn't mean you won't be cast. It just means they have seen all they need to. They may have loved your dancing and know you are perfect for the solo *or* they may want a tall, skinny, exotic-looking person and you're an adorable tiny. Or they have to have ten girls and you're a boy. Or they want someone who dances like their second cousin once removed.

Trivia

Fred Astaire, one of the greatest movie dancers of all time, like every other actor, received his fair share of rejections. When he was first starting out and auditioned for RKO, some genius writing about Fred's screen test said, "Can't act. Slightly bald. Can dance a little."

89

So remember, *getting cast has nothing and everything to do with you.* But if you want to hedge your bets, here's ...

How to Give a Great Dance Audition

Before the Audition Begins

- Bring a water bottle and drink lots of water. It's important to keep your body hydrated.
- Wear tight clothing that allows you to move easily. You want to be able to move freely, but still let the choreographer be able to see your body.
- As Barney the purple dinosaur would sing (if he were a human and a dancer), "warm up, warm up, everybody everywhere, warm up, warm up." But not just your body, you need to warm up your mind.

To Warm Up Your Body

1. *Do upper body stretches.* Stretch the upper arms and shoulders. Stretch the left arm across the front of your body, now hold your upper left arm with your right hand, stretch out the upper left arm for thirty seconds. Reverse arms. Do this two times.

   Stretch the upper sides of your body. Hold your left arm behind your head and pull down the left arm at the elbow with the right hand. Reverse arms. Do this two times.

2. *Do lower body stretches.* Stretch out the legs. Do leg lunges. While keeping your left leg straight, toe pointed forward, heel straight back, step forward with the right leg, and stretch the hamstring. Hold the stretch for a count of thirty seconds. Do two of these on each side.

To Warm Up Your Mind

The point of warming up your mind is to build your confidence. Remember, dancing isn't just about the movement. It's about expressing either the feelings of the character or the feelings inside you. And you need to be focused. There are lots of mental exercises you can do to center yourself.

1. As you're warming up your body, think about performing; the enjoyment of dancing. Think about every time someone said, "Good job."

2. You can think about past shows and the choreography you had then, seeing yourself successfully completing the routine before a thrilled audience.

Once the Audition Starts

1. *Relate with the other dancers when it's appropriate.* We're not talking deep, meaningful conversation, but a "good job" or a well-placed, "Hey!" is always good. Remember, like the director, choreographers have eagle eyes — they see everything. And they want to know you're going to be pleasant to other members of the company and you're easy to work with.
2. *If you make a mistake, don't stop!* So many dancers eliminate themselves by stopping. Keep going. Just like any other performance, you must go on.
3. *Don't try to show off ... unless they ask you to.* Another faux pas by many a dancer is they want to show what they can do so they twist and turn and do double pirouettes, but they end up banging into someone. Ouch! If the dance captain gives you a chance to strut your stuff, which is usually at the last eight counts, that's when you show those extra special things you can do.

Getting Cast as a Dancer

First, yay for you! Wow. That's amazing. And in honor of this momentous event, may I present to you ...

Uh-Huh I'm BAD! You bad. Uh-huh. Mark this day on the calendar in the back.

Rehearsals

Just like being in a straight play, the first thing you will do is a table read. Follow this book's very smart rules of actor etiquette: don't text, be quiet, ask questions, bring a pencil ... you know the drill.

The second thing that will happen is you will be given a schedule. Rehearsals for a musical can be anywhere from three to two to six weeks; depends on the show. Just like actors and singers, dancer rehearsals focus on learning the dances.

Dance Shoes

You will need dance shoes. Which shoes you will need depends on the show — ask the dance captain. You can get shoes at any costume shop or dance shop. Sometimes the production will even give you the shoes. Again, ask! Girls typically need ballet and sometimes toe shoes, character shoes, jazz shoes, jazz sneakers, or tap shoes. Boys typically need jazz shoes, jazz sneakers, or ballet flats.

During Rehearsals

Sometimes the director will work with you and other times not. It's up to you, either way, to create a character for every scene you're in. As a dancer, you might have no lines, lucky you, less to memorize. Find the emotional undercurrent of the score and let the music be your guide. Or study the lyrics of the songs and let the words tell you about your character. Or listen to the rhythm of the music and use that to build your performance.

The fun of being chorus is that you get to play many different roles. You're not locked into one. In *My Fair Lady*, for example, you could be a Cockney shoe shiner in one scene and a high falootin' British dude in another. And with each role you get to create a new story, new feelings and emotions that suit that character and you get to relate to the other characters onstage differently. Fun!

As a dancer, you might be given lines, lucky you. You are given more to work with. Approach your role as an actor. Answer those ever important actor questions:

- Who is your character?
- What is your character's intention?
- Where is your character coming from?
- How does your character feel about the other characters?

In addition, just like singing, figure out why your character needs to dance. Like singing, dance is an exaggerated expression of the character. So why does your character have to dance when walking would do? What makes it that important you have to dance it?

Commitment

You will never get this moment again. So, take advantage, my lovely. For whatever you do, give it your all. Surrender heart and soul. Every moment is a gift — that's why they call it the present.

 **GOLD STAR**

For dancing and singing with everything you had. Yay for you! Go to the back of the book, color a stone. Any color you like. It's your star.

Chapter Ten

Rehearsals

"This is not a tough job. You read a script. If you like the part and the money is OK, you do it. Then you remember your lines. You show up on time. You do what the director tells you to do. When you finish, you rest and then go on to the next part. That's it."
— *Robert Mitchum*

The Director

Every show can have only one guiding force. Think about it. You have a vision, but so does everyone else in the cast. And most of the time they are not the same. So if each of you were free to insist on envisaging what you see, you'd end up with a big old mess of a show. This is why there can only be one person at the helm — the director. And he must have one vision. It is up to you the actor to support that vision as best you can.

What Is Your Place in the Overall Picture?

To find your place in the director's vision, follow his direction. Do as he asks. You can do this by asking yourself these four questions: what is the style of the show, what is the purpose of my character, what is the purpose of this scene, what is the intention of this line as it relates to the scene.

What Is the Style of the Show?

The type of show matters 'cause it gives you an idea of the style of your approach: romantic comedy, period drama, investigative.

Romantic comedies tend to rely a lot on quick, snappy dialogue; pacing has to be quick and fast. A *physical comedy* means you need to focus on the physical gags, making sure they are clean. But a *drama* might mean you need to slow down in certain spots. The director should tell you the style he wants (heaven help him if he doesn't ...).

Flip was working with a director we'll call Riley. Riley didn't know about the director having a vision thing. Rehearsals were spent blocking and re-blocking and then re-blocking again. That's all the actor's did. There was no character work. No pacing. Just re-blocking. Eventually the actors got so frustrated they met in secret, working the show on their own. The production was a disaster.

What Is the Purpose of My Character?

Every character serves a purpose in the greater good of the story. Timon and Pumba are comedic sidekicks to Simba in *The Lion King*. Rizo is the darker side of teen angst in *Grease*. If a character steps beyond their purpose, it can ruin a show.

Flip and I were so excited to write the sequel to *Beauty and the Beast*. Oh wow. We would get to fulfill a childhood dream by being part of the Disney magic. And we would get to not only write a story for such beloved characters as Belle and the Beast but also create some new characters. Lucky us!

Oh be careful what you wish for.

We created a new character for the movie named Fife. A little throw away character that would make the evil villain less scary to children. That was his whole purpose — bad guy not so frightening.

Not according to the director. He fell in love with Fife. He saw so much more for Fife that he asked us to rewrite the script, giving Fife more to do. We argued. But the director had his way. And Fife became a very important character to the movie. Ouch. By doing this, everything changed, including the heart of the piece.

It's important you know the purpose for your character and stick to it.

What Is the Purpose of this Scene?

As you must know the purpose of your character, you need to know the purpose of each scene within the show. Some scenes are expositional like the classroom scene following the incredible action opening of *Raiders of the Lost Ark*. Other scenes are simply there to relieve the audience's tension after some gut-wrenching emotional reveals in the previous scene. By knowing this as an actor, you have a direction to take your character.

We were doing our musical *Wild Dust* (available through Samuel French) and the actress playing the role of Marion had a line following a pretty heavy reveal from another character. She could go one of two ways. Play the line sympathetic, which was perfectly right because Marion truly felt for the other character's pain. Or she could take one for the show and play the irony and humor of the line. Lottie wanted to go for sympathy. But the director in me knew we needed the laugh. What a challenge it was for her to find the motivation to go ironic in that moment. But she did it. And the audience loved her for it. You could practically hear them saying, "Thank you, I needed that" within the peals of laughter. The scene had been so dramatic the audience needed the comedy to release some of the tension. Without it, the show would topple into soap opera territory and we would lose the audience.

What Is the Intention of this Line as it Relates to the Scene?

Each scene has purpose and so does each line. Even if you're stuck in expositional mire, you must make sure you understand everything you are saying and why you are saying it and deliver it with authority. No confusion in you and the poor audience will be able to follow along.

Gates McFadden is the actress who played Dr. Beverly Crusher in *Star Trek: The Next Generation* series. The actress was interviewed about all the medical mumbo jumbo she had to spill out every episode. Wasn't it boring to talk about that stuff? Did she really have to research that gunk? Her answer pleased me. She said she had to know, because oftentimes it was the whole reason for the crew's mission and without her understanding, the audience would be lost. Wow, talk about knowing your place in the overall story.

Your place in the overall scheme of things answered, it's time to get up on your feet and start doing. The mistake that most actors make is they fail to give their all during rehearsals. They mark time until the show opens. This is not a good way to work. Directors need actors to put it all on the line, otherwise they don't know if you understand their notes and can't do them, or don't understand and the director needs to try something else. At Showdown we ask our actors to ...

Dare to Suck

Daring to suck is pushing yourself, taking risks. To dare to suck means to be willing to make mistakes with the intention of creating a more wondrous performance for the audience.

Did you see how I added those last three words? *For the audience.* That phrase is key. Because as much as you want to grow and evolve, in the end you are doing this to entertain, enlighten, and move an audience ... hopefully not out the door. Even if you're a film actor, in the end, you are there for an audience.

So many young actors come through Showdown's doors educated in technique and methods and approaches, yet they weren't loud enough, they mumbled, they took pauses you could drive a truck through, they failed to take direction. These young thespians had no idea what acting was all about. You are creating for an audience. You are emoting for the people who have paid money to see you. You are doing everything you do for the enjoyment of someone else. And it doesn't matter how much emotion you put into that role or how many hours you spent connecting with that character inside you, if the audience doesn't get it, can't hear it, or doesn't care, it's pointless. Oh ouch. That's a hard nut to swallow, isn't it? You are being asked to explore who you are, learn everything about yourself just so you can give it away. But please remember your talent is a gift, and gifts are most enjoyed when they are shared.

From Rehearsals to Final Dress

Remembering that directors differ, I begin with traffic patterns. *Traffic patterns* are the entrances and exits and general places an actor will stand in a scene. Once the show has traffic, my next step is ...

A Stumble Through

A *stumble through* is exactly like it sounds: run a scene, mistakes and all. But at a stumble through, I ask that my actors give me performance-level performances. They *dare to suck.* By doing that I can then know where the holes are and who needs more work.

Stumble through completed, I might give notes, I might not. It depends on how much the actors remember. If they forgot almost everything we worked on, no notes. Back to square one. If they retained, then notes and we run again. Once we've done a bit of shading of performances in the stumble through, it's time for ...

The Stop and Start

In a *stop and start,* a scene is run a bazillion times to make sure that every detail is fully realized in an actor's performance. Oh for example, an actor is to enter USL (upstage left) and run to the couch, breathless. I've told the actor to take a beat before she speaks, but the actor keeps forgetting. Aaaach! In a stop and start, I will run that little bit over and over until the actor remembers. Another thing I might do in a stop and start is work pacing. A scene may need to run fast fast fast and the actors are slow slow slow. We'd run it over and over until the actors can run the scene quickly.

Actor Tips During Stop and Starts

Because acting isn't the only thing happening at this point in the production — the costumer is doing his costumey thing, prop person is acquiring props, set slowly rises — it's easy for actors to forget their actor stuff. To help keep you focused on your performance work, what follows is an actor's checklist.

1. *Projection and diction.* Who's your buddy? Who's your pal? Your diaphragm is! That's right, and that trusty muscle will help you be loud without straining your voice. Remember to check you're supporting your breath often.
2. *Props and costumes.* Don't wait for someone else to bring in props or costumes. If you can provide a "stunt" prop or "stand-

in" costume, go for it. You need to work with a gun, get a toy gun at the dollar store. If you are doing a period piece, work in a long skirt and heels (this will affect posture), and by the time you're in dress rehearsals, you will know how to rise and sit without stepping on your skirt.

3. *Scene Not a Scene.* How many young actors — and old — keep their distance from other actors? It's actually fascinating. The actor is supposed to be confessing his love to his lady and he's ten feet away. I have created a very simple shorthand to remind actors to enter another's personal space. It's called Scene Not a Scene.

   Scene Not a Scene is essentially standing close enough to your partner. You exchange energy. How do you know you've done this? When you move into that space, they will shift in some way. Maybe their back will stiffen or they'll lean back. Your purpose is not to offend them, but to challenge them energetically. Creative tension is a good thing. It creates a kind of chemistry.

   One last thought about knowing to scene not a scene. If you choose to stand away from your partner, it's a choice. The distance now has meaning because you've chosen to stand far away.

4. *Geometric Patterns.* Something about actors and lines: they love to create lines. Squiggly, straight, meandering lines. Well I want you to say "no" to lines! That's right, say it now, "no lines!" Whenever you are told to go near someone on a stage, avoid standing in a line. Think geometric shapes. If there's three of you go triangle, four can make a diamond. Remember your silhouettes?

5. *Relationships.* Everyone on that stage has a relationship with your character. It's up to you to define that relationship and work it. Is this person your estranged father, your beloved sister, your annoying neighbor? And when you pass them or stand near them, remember that relationship.

6. *Don't pretend to talk or relate. Just talk or relate.* If you're supposed to have a chat with someone, figure out what that chat is about. What is your intention for the chat? Now have that chat. Do it quietly with little movement if you're not the focus of the scene, but do it for real.

7. *Plant your feet.* Don't rock back and forth, you're not a metronome. You're a human.

8. *Unless you have reason to move, don't.* And if you are told to move, give intention and purpose to it. Find a reason to move!

9. *Get off book as quickly as possible.* Getting off book is exactly as it sounds, you stop using the script. This enables you to free up

your hands and mind to live more in the moment. Word of warning here: if you're not ready to be off book, don't try to be. It's OK to wait until you feel you have a clean command of your lines and blocking, 'cause otherwise you waste valuable rehearsal time asking for lines.

10. *Ask for lines.* When off book, all you need say is "line." Not "I'm sorry, I thought I knew this." Or "What's that again? Are you sure?" Just say "line" and be done with it.

11. *Write it down.* I'll say it again, *write it down.* Whatever the director tells you are pearls of wisdom and you need to write it down. And then when you aren't in rehearsal, review what was said and give it some thought.

12. *Never show up at rehearsal without pencil and script.* Enough said, right?

13. *Don't give another actor direction. Ever!* Oh my, it's considered really bad form. And can irritate a director to no end. If an actor asks you for feedback, tell that actor you don't really feel it's your place and tell that actor to talk to the director.

Super busy, you need to make sure you're taking time for you. How's about a blended freeze from Sonic or a nice bright, apple? I love McIntosh, but you pick whatever you like.

With these tips now firmly implanted in your performance, it's time to get out of stumble through land and enter the world of ...

Dress Rehearsals

(Cue deep ominous music sting) Dress rehearsals are also known as ... dum dum dum! ... *hell week.* No really, that's what dress rehearsals are called ... dum dum dum! ... *hell week.* And there's a reason they are called ... dum dum dum! ... *hell week.* It's that time in the show when costumes, sets, props, and actors all come together in a ... screaming hysterical mishmash of doubt that this show should ever go up. I have seen sane actors lose it, actors walk into the orchestra pit, and actors quit. It's so intense, it should actually be a reality series: "Fifteen actors. One show! Who will survive on ... dum dum dum! ... *Hell Week?*"

All kidding aside … sort of … actors are tired from lack of sleep and overwork. It's really important to take good care. So take heart oh young one and take heed, here are some of Cindy's Hell Week Survival Tips.

1. *Be good to yourself.* Say "no!" Why is it that when we are most overworked we add more stuff to do? If this sounds familiar, "Oh, it's dress rehearsals, I can type that paper for you and clean the house and bake cookies for the school fair," then it's time to say, "No!" For this week, keep extra stuff down to a minimum.

2. *Get sleep.* Shut off the iPod, the computer, and the TV and go to bed early at least one night.

3. *Eat somewhat healthy.* Opt away from the creamy coffee stuff and head towards the real fruit stuff. Add some carrots to those French fries. Throw in a glass of water or seven.

4. *Say at least one nice thing to yourself.* Before you go to sleep, think of one thing that you did great. Was it you sang really loud? Or you didn't hit your little brother when you wanted to? Or you got a passing grade on that math exam? You rock and you need to remember that.

5. *Enjoy this as much as you can.* Life isn't a dress rehearsal, my lovely. You don't get to come back down this way again, so savor it. Have fun. Let yourself get silly. Or laugh. Or just take a moment and recognize what joy this is.

6. *And last, but not least, please accept this award.*

 **GOLD STAR**

For sticking to it. Yay for you! Go to the back of the book, color a stone. Any color you like. It's your star.

Continuing to Grow Your Character

Actors tend to feel lost during hell week, because the director is so distracted by the myriad of other stuff that needs doing: lights have to be set and cues run, costumes need to be checked and changed as needed, sets might or might not need repair, props and prop tables make an appearance, then there's selling tickets, making programs, and whatever other details go into making a show. Director's notes seem to be all about the technical stuff, and not about performance. But no worries, you can stay on track even if the director's mind seems a million miles away. Be you in a musical or straight play, *stay in character.*

At Showdown, the chant is "Where does the character begin? Offstage! When does the character end? Never!" Now we don't really mean never, but in the reality of the show world, you must not drop character until the end of the run-through. Even if the director is giving you notes, take notes in character. Think, "How would my character react to being in a show and having a director give notes?"

Daniel Roebuck is a well-known character actor. You have seen him in everything, including *Lost*. He played the physical science teacher who gets blown up by the crappy dynamite. He's wonderful. And every time he comes onscreen he's different. What is totally neat is that from the onset, Daniel never drops his character. He played the mayor in our movie *Jack and the Beanstalk* and by goodness if Mr. R wasn't the mayor the whole entire time. It was really cool. Whenever you'd come up to him and ask a question, even if it was completely unrelated to the movie, Daniel would answer like his character — accent and all!

So now, at Showdown, when the actors don't stay in character, we say WWDD? What would Daniel do? Hey, if it's good enough for Daniel, a *working* actor, it's good enough for you!

Louder, Faster, Funnier

This is a chant we teach Showdown actors, "Louder, faster, funnier!" And it means exactly what it sounds like. Be your loudest. Pick up your cues. And find the comedy whenever possible.

Ah, the comedy. We take life way too seriously. I believe audiences hunger for genuine laughter. It helps us to forget our troubles. And it helps us to stay engaged in a show. Laughter is the release valve. Without it, audiences will tune out. They need the relief. Find the humor!

"I'm an assistant storyteller. It's like being a waiter or a gas-station attendant, but I'm waiting on six million people a week, if I'm lucky."
— Harrison Ford, on being an actor

Final Dress Rehearsal Notes

Remember pacing. I've seen good shows with talented companies die a horrible death because actors did not pick up their cues. Actors took endless pauses thinking they were being deep when all they were doing was adding misery to the audience. Pick up your cues! Cut out the time between the lines. Think about any conversation you've ever had. You jump on what other people say, you interrupt, you speak out of turn. Conversations have energy in real life and the same thing needs to apply for stage.

The Shotgun Game

Purpose of the game:
Clear out the pauses between actors' lines.

Directions:
1. Have someone on book, listening.
2. Actors pace, and I mean pace, quick, staccato steps across the stage.
3. While pacing, actors run through their lines.
4. The person on book listens for pauses between the lines and poor diction. If an actor has even a breath between lines or cannot be understood, actors repeat that section until they get it right. Actors will go again and again, as many times as need be, to gut those pauses.

All or Nothin'

Will from *Oklahoma* could not have said it better. When running a run-through, it's all or nothin' for you. You must work at full performance level. Don't hold back. Hopefully you've been giving it your all for quite some time. But if you haven't, for whatever reason, it's put up or shut up time. And if you find yourself holding back, I have to wonder why. What are you waiting for? Right here, right now, commit to giving it everything you have. Whatever *it* is: that soccer game, school paper, job at McDonald's, speech, or baby-sitting. You deserve that. And so does the world. You are amazing and for all time there will never be another you. *Show up.* Give it everything you have. You don't want to wake up tomorrow and say, "woulda, coulda, shoulda." Truly, there is no other moment than this one. So live it fully. No retreat, no surrender, and no regrets.

Uh-Huh I'm BAD! You bad. Uh-huh. Mark this day on the calendar in the back.

Chapter Eleven

Performance

> "The thing about performance, even if it's only an illusion,
> is that it is a celebration of the fact that we do contain
> within ourselves infinite possibilities."
> — Daniel Day Lewis

Another opening, another show ...
You made it through casting, callbacks, rehearsals, and more. You are about to perform for the audience, but before you go on ...

Just a Few Last Minute Notes

1. Warm up your voice.
2. Warm up your body.
3. Warm up your mind.
4. Have a light meal. Enough to keep your energy up but not so much you feel weighed down. Carbs are good.
5. Have plenty of water available. It's good to keep a water bottle in the dressing room and on both sides of the stage.
6. If you don't have a prop master, set your props. And if you do, double-check that your props are where they're supposed to be.
7. Use the nerves, don't fight them. You're excited. Let it build your energy.
8. From the moment you start getting into makeup, shed yourself and become your character. Let the world you're creating for the audience encompass you.
9. Commit fully. Show up!
10. Enjoy, my lovely.

A Technical Note

Hold for laughs. Laughter comes in waves. It starts as a giggle or snortle and then it builds from one person to several to sometimes the entire crowd. Bigger and bigger it gets. Then it starts to fade. As it came in, it rolls out. You never want to jump on a laugh. If you do, the audience, afraid to miss something, will stop laughing. This is bad. We want them to laugh. Laughter is good. So you have to time your next line delivery at just the right point in the laughter wave. You have to "work" your audience. After laughter has begun, you wait, enjoy the laughter, then just as it's beginning to die down, you deliver the next line. Don't let the laughter go silent. That's bad too 'cause it sucks the energy out of the show.

The Run of the Show

So you did it! Your show opened. How was it? What did you think? How do you feel? Oh wait, I have something for you ...

Yay! *Clap clap clap.* Bravo! You rock.

But before you go on, I want you to take a moment. Think back to the throes of hell week when you felt like the show would never come together, you might have doubted that you could actually pull it off. Remember that? Now leap back to today. How do you feel? Pretty great, huh? You feel accomplished or proud or on top of the world? That's because you showed up, my lovely. You gave the show your all! And you did do it! You!

Now ask yourself, "If I did this, and I didn't think I could do it, what else could I do? Could I really go to Harvard? Could I ask that guy out? Could I become a Broadway dancer?" Hmmmm.

So now that we've celebrated opening night ...

You are the total star of the night. Eat whatever you darn well please. A banana split. A super macchiato with double whip. Chili fries. The world is your oyster, baby!

Second Night Slump

'Tis a common ailment, in theatre land, after the highs of opening night are the lows of the second night performance. To defeat this evil monster that can suck the joy out of a show in nothing flat, I have one thing to say to you … *stay in character!*

And remember, there is no such thing as a bad audience, no matter how much you may try to pass off your low energy on them. Sorry. Audiences are not ever bad. If they're not responding to you, it's because you are holding back. You need to give more. And if you're having trouble doing that, imagine that there's someone in the audience that's really important to you. Someone you dearly cherish. Now imagine you are giving your performance for them.

The Final Curtain

Oh sad face, the show is over. It's time to call it a night. But before you leave, there are just a few more things you need to know.

The Strike

After the last performance it's time to clear the theatre of your set. And put away or return props and costumes. *Everybody,* and I *mean everybody,* (if it's not a union show) must participate in this ritual. You too! No excuses. I don't care who is waiting for you. They will wait longer. It takes a company to create a show and it takes a company to put it away.

Look at the strike as closure. You're putting everything away, returning what must be returned so you can move on with your life. How cool is that to be able to put closure on this experience? I can count on one hand the amount of times I've actually got to have closure in relationships that meant a lot to me. But with a strike, I can do this. Strikes may not look it, but they are wonderful to help you go on.

Saying Good-Bye

When a show ends, it's like a part of you dies too, especially those shows that are an amazing experience where everything clicked. With those misery monsters, it's hard to say good-bye. And so there is nothing I can say to that except being sad is part of the process.

Many an actor will promise to stay in touch. And at the time they say that, those actors mean it. But lives get busy and warmth fades. Just know that the love behind the words never goes away. You'll meet up with that actor again and suddenly you'll both be filled with a gush of joy. Or you won't see them again. And that's OK too. 'Cause the love doesn't disappear. It's always there. And funny thing about love, the more you give of it, the more there is to give. So give it freely.

Chapter Twelve

What Jane Jenkins Says

Jane and her partner Janet Hirschenson run The Casting Company. Together they have discovered the likes of Tom Cruise, Patrick Swayze, Rob Lowe, and the list goes on and on. In addition, they cast for some of the biggest directors in Hollywood including Ron Howard. Some of the films they have cast are *Harry Potter and the Sorcerer's Stone, Angels & Demons,* and some of the James Bond movies.

As casting directors, Jane and Janet's job is to cast the movie. Once the script is in shooting shape, they work with the director and producer in creating a list of actors they would like to see for the bigger roles. Jane and Janet then "go after" those actors, making an offer to the actor's agent or manager. Jane and Janet don't determine the offer, that's decided by the overall film budget. In addition, they will bring in actors to read for the smaller parts. These actors come into their office and their audition is videotaped. The director looks at the videos and decides who he wants. Jane and Janet will make recommendations, but in the end, it's the director's call.

I love talking to Jane. She is smart and kind and honest and I always walk away from my conversations feeling empowered. Her ability to make me feel good about myself is a rare gift in anyone, particularly anyone in Hollywood. It also explains why she is an in-demand casting director.

I had lots of questions for Jane. Here they go …

Cindy: When you are looking for an actor, what are you looking for?
Jane: Someone who can play the action and make choices, uses the lines to accomplish an objective. And take direction.
Cindy: So intention is key. And if that intention is in conflict with the director's intention for the character, the actor must be able to change their intention.

Cindy: If every actor has a unique quality, how do they find what that unique quality is?
(Jane's answer was twofold. It began by her talking about her own personal experience and then morphed into how that affects how she looks at actors.)
Jane: Initially, we believe that we are all unique. We know we all have

different abilities and different tastes. I might like salty, you like sweet. I can play the drums you can do algebra, but we somehow underestimate that uniqueness. We think, "Yeah, but what I have to offer is no big deal, anyone could do this." Then as we grow and mature, we come to understand that no, other people can't do this as well as I do. I just know there are things I'm capable of. It's a maturing process.

When I look at an actor, I don't actually know them. It's a superficial connection. So yes, I know there are qualities that are unique to them, but I don't know what they are. What I see is what they present. Are they intrinsically interesting? Can they hold a conversation? Do they have something interesting to say? Are they observant? Or funny? Am I engaged in what they have to speak about?

If you're so shy that nothing can be brought out of you, then you probably should not become an actor. But if you're conscious of being shy, you know that's a quality you possess, then work towards opening yourself up.

If you are an interested person, you will be interesting. Inform yourself as to what is going on in the universe. What you're passionate about, intro that into your conversations with people.

Cindy: So we really do need to know who we are. Not only does that give us more to bring to the table as actors, as people it gives us something to share. I love the comment about knowing your unique gifts. It's OK to believe we are special. We each have something wonderful to offer.

Cindy: So when an actor comes in to read for you, you are just as much interested in who they are as what they're reading?

Jane: There are two kinds of auditions. They come in and read. And [there's] a General.

In a General, the actors come in but they're not there to read for a specific role.

Cindy: You are just there to meet them.

Jane: For example, I had two actors come in. One of them I'd seen his video, so I knew he could act. The purpose was to meet him and get to know him. I ask him questions about himself. Where did the actor come from? How will he answer?

Does he say something like, "I became an actor 'cause my mom and dad wanted me to"? Which is terribly uninteresting. Or will he say, "I became an actor because my mom and dad wanted me to. I was this difficult child with lots of energy who wrote on the walls and they needed to channel my energy." One answer is just sort of generic. The other is interesting. There are details.

Cindy: So being interesting, is that giving details?

Jane: If it's interesting to you, then it will probably be interesting to someone else.

Cindy: So a non-general audition would be like a casting call. You have a part in mind and actors come in to read for that. There isn't much time for chitchat, it's just basically, hello, how are you, and they read.

Cindy: What happens when they read for you?

Jane: When actors are starting out, they're probably going to come for the one and two line roles. They will come in and I'll chat with them for a minute or two and then they will read for me. It really depends on the size of the part. These smaller, one and two lines, I take about five minutes, tops.

Cindy: In such a short time, how does an actor make an impression?

Jane: I want to be engaged.

I was casting a part for a movie. A young woman. A super model at a car show. She had two lines. Something about the new taillights of the car. And then a guy asks, "So you only do this 'cause, why?" "Because I get paid." Two lines. And of the ten people who came in and read, nine of the readings were blah. They made it nothing. But the girl I hired made me laugh. She found the humor. She made something of those two lines. She took a beat. She found the humor.

I was engaged.

Cindy: But with two lines, how do you make something of them? How do you create a character?

Jane: First you read the script. The scene is set up. You understand the kind of movie. It's not my business to teach you how to act. You need to know how to do that. But you need to know what kind of movie it is. Is it a comedy? A drama?

Cindy: So the style of the story really does matter and actors need to know whether this is a crime drama, a bold comedy, or a chick flick.

Jane: And you have an attitude.

We were casting a customs inspector. A guy that stamps your passport. And our leading lady comes up to him and says something about being a bit superstitious and would the customs agent wish her good luck. So he says, "Good luck."

The director saw 117 actors for those two words. 117 actors. And the guy he cast was the guy who got the joke. Now I thought, there were a few who could have done it. But the director was looking for that something.

It's better if you get the script, but most times all you'll get are these few lines and you have to make a decision to make it interesting. Decide how your character views the world, do something with it.

Cindy: Can you ask your agent about the script?

Jane: The agent should have it. Or have read it. You can talk to the receptionist when you come in. Or you can ask the casting director.

Cindy: Can you ask the casting director days before the reading what this is about?

Jane: Well, when you come in you can say, "What's this movie about?" "What's going on?" You can wait till the last minute 'cause it's a line or two and you will already have it memorized.

Cindy: So actors should memorize the side?

Jane: Yes.

Cindy: Earlier you mentioned taking a beat, you can't do that in stage, can you?

Jane: You can take a breath. The difference between stage and film is in stage everything is heightened. In film you have a microphone two inches above your head. You keep it simple and quiet.

Cindy: Any advice you'd give an actor?

Jane: Have fun.

Cindy: What about dealing with disappointment? Discouragement? 'Cause you're going to be discouraged, right?

Jane: Odds are.

You want to know why you're doing this. Are you looking to be Miley Cyrus next week or are you in it for the long haul? Like Jody Foster.

Jody Foster was also a child actor but she went on to have a life career, be a director. Ron Howard, he's now an award winning director.

Have a bigger picture and remember it. Stick to that big picture.

Cindy: Don't take the rejections personally?

Jane: It's hard not to take them personally. It feels personal. Your every hope and desire hangs on that audition. But it's not personal, we have ten people come in and there's only one job.

I don't even know you so it can't be personal.

Have a vision and stick to it.

If it were easy, everyone would do it.

Have the courage of your convictions and remember to keep the big picture in mind.

Chapter Thirteen

Some Final Thoughts

To become an actor or not to become an actor — that is the question I am most often asked. And the answer I give is, "Do you want to become an actor?" I'm kinda vague, I know, but the truth is, the only person who can tell you what to be is you. You have the power, nobody else.

If You Can Imagine It, You Can Achieve It

When I decided I wanted to become a writer, my boss, who was a high-powered movie exec (and will remain nameless), told me "You will never make it. There are only so many Bill Goldman's in this world and you aren't one of them." Seriously. That's what he said. I think he was trying to protect me. Oh, heaven help us from the "protectors" in our lives. And you want to know my favorite part about my boss' "infinite" wisdom? He hadn't read my script. He had decided this by looking at me.

So I had a choice. I could listen to his opinion of me or I could do an end-run around him. I could sell my screenplay to someone else, which, by the way, is what I did. I sold that screenplay to Paramount. Ha!

Boy, was he mad. I created quite a stir in that company 'cause here we were a movie producing entity and I sold my movie to someone else. Policy changed after I left. Every person who wrote a screenplay at that company had to submit it to development before shopping it anywhere else. Little me changed the way that big company did business.

And you can too. You can become whatever you dream, you just have to believe. It's fortune cookie wisdom, but sometimes the simplest truths are the wisest. So, "Do you want to become an actor?" Then become one.

The Dream Journal

I have a bloody awful time daydreaming. Every time I let myself imagine grand adventures for myself, I get bogged down in the details. Let me give you an example. Currently I daydream about going to Australia. I want to snorkel the Great Barrier Reef, stand front and center in the Sydney Opera House, pet a koala bear, see a jumping kangaroo. So far so good, huh? But then I start to go astray. I think, "Well, how will

I get to Australia?" It costs a fortune to fly there, like $1,500 from L.A. I can't afford that. Then I wonder about getting another job, but then I start to think about how much time that would take away from my writing and all the stuff we need to do around the house, like replace the roof that $1,500 could pay for. Plus there are hotels to pay for when I'm in Australia and car rental and gas and food. My happy little daydream has become a nightmare because I got in there and messed with the details. I overthought the dream instead of just let it be what it was: a daydream. And I bet you do this too. So that's why I recommend you begin keeping a dream journal.

What you will need:
A small spiral notebook
A pen
A vast imagination

Directions:
Whenever the whim hits, record your dreams. Oh, and don't edit. Just let one idea lead to the next. Let go of how you're going to make the dream happen. Use all those lovely senses to really visualize yourself living your dream. Then let it go.

You can get playful with your dream journal. Start collecting the music you will listen to when you are doing the thing you dream. Cut out pics of your dream place or thing from magazines or download them off the Internet. Have fun with this. And then let it go.

Practical Tools

"If you have built castles in the air, your work need not be lost. There is where they should be. Now put foundations under them."
— Henry David Thoreau

So you might be wondering, "Well, if I just dream about what I want to do, what's the point? I mean, I want to make it happen." Of course you do! But thinking about how to manifest a dream and actually taking the steps to manifest a dream are two different things. Let me clarify ...

I dreamed of becoming a screenwriter. *And* I took practical steps to make that happen. I didn't think about the steps till the dream withered away to nothingness, I stepped. I began by doing my homework. I learned my craft by reading every book out there about writing a great movie and then I applied what I learned. I rewrote and rewrote until my first script was the best I could make it. I studied who was where and what they were doing so that I could submit it to the right people when the script was ready. I networked like a nut. I took classes and seminars to understand what was selling and why and how this information could help me make my screenplay better. I read up on different writers, finding role models, and then learned how they got to be successful in hopes that their path might open up a path for me. In other words, I became a working screenwriter 'cause I worked. I ignored the naysayers and fortified myself with lots of TLC (and Ben and Jerry's) when the rejections came. Does this make sense? Dreams come true at the crossroads of perspiration and inspiration. If you want to become an actor, you have to do your homework.

Ten Things You can do to Fulfill Your Actor Dream

1. *Read,* my lovely, anything and everything you can get your hands on. The more educated you are, the more knowledge you will have to bring to your next role.
2. *Study your craft.* Take classes and never stop taking classes. There are so many wonderful things to learn: singing, ballet, jazz, mime, improv, classic acting, commercial acting, stage combat, writing, directing … You see, the list goes on and on.
3. *Work your craft.* It's not enough to take classes, you want to apply what you've learned so audition for shows and student films and commercials. Try casting workshops. And if no role comes your way, then create your own opportunity. Pretend you're Judy Garland and Mickey Rooney and build your own barn and put on your own play.
4. *Find a mentor.* There are actors out there who you admire, right? Well learn about them. The Internet rocks for stuff like this. See how your favorite actor got started. How did they deal with rejection and success? I encourage you to take it one step farther, write them. Tell them about yourself. They may not write you back, but then again, they might. Wouldn't that be cool?
5. *Take risks — smart risks.* You know what I mean. Don't jump off a cliff or take drugs — that's just stupid. You're harming your body and you will age much faster and thereby it will be harder to get work. But fun risks are always a good idea. Try auditioning for singing roles or take an improv class. Push yourself. Step outside that comfort zone and try things you didn't think you could do.
6. *Go to movies and performances of all kinds.* Especially theatre because there is an immediacy with another actor that you don't get with movies. See what other performers are doing. And if

cost is an issue, there's local community theatre. Shakespeare in the park is usually free and you can volunteer to usher or work the box office.

7. *Create a supportive circle of friends.* This is a wonderful tool. Oh my goodness. There is no better way to accomplish your dreams than standing beside the people you love. I mean how many times do you hear about actors saying they got their break from their roommate in college or someone they took classes with? Make friends.

8. *Be kind to yourself.* Collect all the nice notes you've received and read them every once in a while.

9. *Let go.* If you find yourself banging your head against a wall, maybe it's time to walk away. This isn't giving up; this is giving yourself a breather, time to check in and make sure you still want to pursue acting, because maybe you don't. And that's OK too. The important thing is for you to be true to yourself.

10. *Network.* And you can begin by going to my blog: cindymarcusauthor.blogspot.com. Every week I give tips on surviving and having fun while you pursue your actor dream. Leave messages so that other actors can get in touch with you. Read what others are saying. It can inspire or guide you towards an opportunity or just make you feel less alone. But I am not the only networking site. There's also www.showdown stageco.com. That's the Showdown website, also a place to connect with other actors. Google "actor networking" sites for opportunities both locally and internationally.

Do I Go to College?

Wow. That's a tough question I get a lot too. Ha! I have a straight answer for this question and that's, "Yes, go to college."

But don't go to college 'cause you need another profession to fall back on in case you fail as an actor. I don't think prepping for a failure is a reason to do anything.

Go to college because you want to have more opportunity. In college you will learn more, meet people and make friends, work beside future directors and producers and writers and other actors, have wonderful life experiences that will help you to formulate that amazing human you are becoming.

Going to college is fun. Get your degree. It couldn't hurt. Whatever you get your degree in.

The Once and Future You

So when Flip and I were at Disney we went to lots of parties. One of them was a casino thing. We got to bet coins and wear fancy duds. It was really fun. And while we were there we met this neat waiter. We asked him what he wanted to do with his life. We knew he didn't want to be a waiter. See, everyone in Hollywood wants to be an actor or writer or director and they are just earning money at their job until they become an actor or writer or director. Our waiter wanted to be an actor. Flip asked him how he felt about being a waiter. Did it bother him not to be acting but waiting tables? He said, with a smile, "This is my wart experience."

OK, that didn't sound too happy to me. A wart experience? How was acting like having warts? He laughed and explained. He meant Wart from *The Once and Future King* by T. H. White. If you haven't read this book, read it now. Well, after you finish my book. It's wonderful. The story of King Arthur. When he was a boy, he was known as Wart, and Merlin would transform Wart into all different kinds of living beings, from ants to eagles. And with each adventure into another's life, Wart would come to understand his own. It's why he became the legendary king.

Our wonderful waiter viewed being a waiter as his Wart experience. He would commit to this job with everything he had, learn to be the best waiter possible 'cause he knew that somewhere, somehow it would enhance his acting, and vice versa. He was right.

Your Wart Experience

When you go to college, don't be afraid to try different majors. Attend different clubs. Go to games. And commit fully to whatever path you have chosen. Give being an accounting major a spin if it interests you. Go after being pre-law if you fancy yourself an attorney. Go out for a team if you dream of a being a jock. I promise it will only enhance your life.

You see, my lovely, if you are meant to become an actor, it doesn't matter if you are eighteen or eighty-two, major in English or film — you will become an actor.

Final Toast

To you, my lovely, this is just the beginning of your grand and glorious life. Here's to all the mistakes you will make so you can learn that you can fall down and more importantly, get back up again. Gosh you're strong. To the manifestation of all your dreams, may they be as grand and glorious as you.

Silver Latte

A glass of sparkling cider and a big fat piece of chocolate — enjoy!

I'm proud of you. I can't wait to hear about the actor/person you are about to become.

Appendix

GOLD STAR

Sunday	Monday	Tuesday	Wednesday	Thursday	Friday	Saturday

About the Author

Every year the staff of the Teenage Drama Workshop, a teen drama camp with classes and productions, chooses a student who best exemplifies what the program is all about. When Cindy was a teenager, she won an acting scholarship to the Workshop in Los Angeles. She's made her living in show business ever since. With her husband and writing partner Flip Kobler, she spent many years at Disney writing the sequels to *The Lion King*, *Beauty and the Beast*, *Pocahontas*, *Lady and the Tramp*, *Hunchback of Notre Dame*, and many, many others. She is now the front man for Showdown, sharing her unique experience in Hollywood and passion for theatre with a new generation. Showdown is a national teen theatre program, taking teens from insecure and uncertain to empowered and employable. Showdown believes the arts can change young lives for the better. As an in-demand acting coach, she helps craft young actors and as a mentor, she supports young souls. As a writer she continues to have plays published, screenplays sold, and manages her blog, cindymarcusauthor.blogspot.com, but working with young people is her true calling.

This is Cindy's second book with Meriwether Publishing. In *PLAYdate*, she shares her expertise by guiding the novice director through producing a play.

Order Form

Meriwether Publishing Ltd.
PO Box 7710
Colorado Springs, CO 80933-7710
Phone: 800-937-5297 Fax: 719-594-9916
Website: www.meriwether.com

Please send me the following books:

_____ **The Ultimate Young Actors Guide** $19.95
#BK-B324
by Cindy Marcus
Getting the role and making it shine

_____ **PLAYdate #BK-B307** $19.95
by Cindy Marcus
A parent's and teacher's guide to putting on a play

_____ **Acting for Life #BK-B281** $19.95
by Jack Frakes
A textbook on acting

_____ **Acting for Love & Money #BK-B313** $19.95
by Paul G. Gleason and Gavin Levy
Connecting the craft to the industry

_____ **275 Acting Games: Connected #BK-B314** $19.95
by Gavin Levy
A workbook of theatre games for developing acting skills

_____ **112 Acting Games #BK-B277** $17.95
by Gavin Levy
A comprehensive workbook of theatre games

_____ **Improv Ideas #BK-B283** $23.95
by Justine Jones and Mary Ann Kelley
A book of games and lists

These and other fine Meriwether Publishing books are available at
your local bookstore or direct from the publisher. Prices subject to
change without notice. Check our website or call for current prices.

Name: _____ email:_____

Organization name: _____

Address: _____

City: _____ State: _____

Zip: _____ Phone: _____

❏ **Check enclosed**

❏ **Visa / MasterCard / Discover / Am. Express #** _____

Signature: _____   Expiration date: _____ / _____
(required for credit card orders)

Colorado residents: Please add 3% sales tax.
Shipping: Include $3.95 for the first book and 75¢ for each additional book ordered.

❏ *Please send me a copy of your complete catalog of books and plays.*